NOW PLAYING
Learning Communication Through Film

2016 EDITION

Darin Garard

Santa Barbara City College

Heidi Kirkman

Howard Community College

D1511204

New York   Oxford

Oxford University Press

Oxford University Press is a department of the University of Oxford.
It furthers the University's objective of excellence in research,
scholarship, and education by publishing worldwide.

Oxford New York
Auckland   Cape Town   Dar es Salaam   Hong Kong   Karachi
Kuala Lumpur   Madrid   Melbourne   Mexico City   Nairobi
New Delhi   Shanghai   Taipei   Toronto

With offices in
Argentina   Austria   Brazil   Chile   Czech Republic   France   Greece
Guatemala   Hungary   Italy   Japan Poland   Portugal   Singapore
South Korea   Switzerland   Thailand   Turkey   Ukraine   Vietnam

For titles covered by Section 112 of the US Higher Education
Opportunity Act, please visit www.oup.com/us/he for the
latest information about pricing and alternate formats.

Published by Oxford University Press
198 Madison Avenue, New York, New York 10016
http://www.oup.com

Oxford is a registered trademark of Oxford University Press

ISBN: 978-0-19-049909-9

Printing number: 9 8 7 6 5 4 3 2 1

Printed in the United States of America
on acid-free paper

CONTENTS

Section III: Full-Length Feature Films...... 52

Section IV: Feature Film Websites of Interest......... 99

Index by Communication Concepts *100*

INTRODUCTION

Communication is a human necessity—without it, we could scarcely coexist. Observing and analyzing communication patterns, interactions, and the many other intricacies of human contact is how we learn to project ourselves more effectively. Oftentimes it is difficult to evaluate our own communication processes in an objective manner—but watching people communicating in films can be an excellent way to identify and understand many aspects of communication. Closely watching others engaged in communication on film can help bring theories and concepts to life.

This manual contains sections on **Feature Film Scenes** and **Television Programs**—a variety of specific scenes that illustrate the good, the bad, and the ugly of human interaction, along with discussion questions for each scene. A third section, **Full-Length Feature Films,** provides examples of entire films that provide insights into human communication, with a detailed synopsis of the movie along with discussion questions to prompt critical thinking.

Looking at the various characters in these films struggle with communication can be liberating as well as enlightening—we can observe it from a distance and, without being too self-conscious, pick up on both the good and the bad habits that can lead us to become better communicators. Have fun learning!

SECTION I
FEATURE FILM SCENES

Each of the entries in this section is a "stand alone" scene that illustrates communication concepts (with a strong focus on interpersonal communication). The scenes are listed in alphabetical order by film title; they are also arranged by category in the index at the end of the book. The time locations of the scenes are measured from the opening moment of the movie, just after the display of the film company (in other words, don't begin counting on your timer until all the previews on the video are finished).

Film: *50/50*
Year: 2011
Central Concept: Listening
Related Concepts: Social Support, Barriers to Effective Listening, Disconfirmation

Length and Location of Scene #1: Approximately 2 minutes (Chapter 2: 0:07:55–0:10:15)
Opening Line: "Hi."
Closing Line: "Now as I said, you should consider. . . ."
Length and Location of Scene #2: Approximately 1 minute (Chapter 3: 0:11:10–0:11:54)
Opening Line: "Oh Adam."
Closing Line: "Yeah, it will be okay. Alright?"
Length and Location of Scene #3: Approximately 2 minutes (Chapter 3: 0:11:55–0:13:50)
Opening Line: "I'm gonna throw up."
Closing Line: "I'm awake now."

Scene Descriptions: At 27 years old, Adam (Joseph Gordon-Levitt) has a fairly normal life: he lives with his girlfriend Rachel (Bryce Dallas Howard), he works at a public radio station as a program writer, and his best friend Kyle (Seth Rogen) is often obnoxious. After a routine medical checkup, however, Adam is diagnosed with a rare form of spinal cancer and given 50/50 odds of survival—hence the film's title. While Adam battles his cancer through chemotherapy and surgery, he experiences a number of different reactions from people once they learn about his condition.

Here are three scenes that illustrate different listening styles in response to Adam's diagnosis. Although each scene could stand alone, watching all three works very well to compare and contrast the characters' reactions to Adam's news. In the first scene, Adam's physician focuses on explaining the technical details of Adam's cancer and completely ignores the relational dimension of the message. In scene two, Rachel provides a supportive and comforting shoulder for Adam to lean on; watching the entire film, however, reveals Rachel's true colors. And in the third scene, when Kyle learns about the cancer, he reacts even more dramatically than Adam did; Kyle also provides advice that seems less than helpful. Taken together, these three scenes show how empathy and social support are necessary skills for competent communication. Indeed, at some point we each find ourselves in situations where others need our support.

Discussion Questions:

1. In Scene #1 Adam hears his diagnosis is cancer, but he immediately stops listening. Identify the causes of Adam's poor listening in this context. In this situation, is it possible for Adam to have been a better listener?

2. Describe how Adam's physician broke the news to Adam in Scene #1. How could he have been more supportive and empathetic? Role play the situation in Scene #1 where you are the physician and someone else is Adam, and talk in a way that practices supportive communication.

3. Compare and contrast Rachel's responses in Scene #2 with Kyle's reactions in Scene #3. What does Rachel do that shows support? What does Kyle do? Are they both effective supportive listeners? Why or why not?

4. Thinking about Rachel and Kyle, are there inherent gender differences in providing social support to others? When you need support, do you seek out a male or a female? Why?

Film: *Almost Famous*
Year: 2000
Central Concept: Self-Disclosure
Related Concepts: Identity Management, Group Communication
Approximate Scene Location: 96 minutes into the 122-minute movie
Approximate Scene Length: 4 minutes
Opening Line: Brief shot of plane flying through storm (no dialogue)
Closing Line: "Thank God we're all alive. We're going to make it!" (To capture facial expressions of the passengers after they realize they will survive, don't cut until scene ends, about 10 seconds after last line of dialogue.)

Scene Description: A 1970s rock band is on tour when its plane is caught in a violent storm. The prospect of imminent death moves several members of the group and its entourage to reveal facts and feelings they had previously kept to themselves. Some of the self-disclosing messages are positive; others are upsetting and disruptive. The scene offers a good foundation for exploring several dimensions of self-revelation: reasons for opening up, the conditions under which disclosure is likely to occur, and the risks and benefits of candor. **Note: The scene contains language that may offend some viewers.**

Discussion Questions:

1. Place the self-disclosures offered in this scene on a continuum, ranging from "appropriate under most conditions" to "inappropriate under most conditions." Describe the conditions under which the disclosures might be appropriate or inappropriate.

2. Which members of the group have been engaging in high levels of identity management with the others? What will happen to the management of their identities now that they've made these revelations?

3. Describe the following group communication concepts at work in this scene: ripple effect, conformity, openness, and boundaries.

4. Have you ever made a self-disclosure in a group of people that you later regretted? Discuss why you made the disclosure and how you managed your identity in later interactions with those people.

Film: *American Sniper*
Year: 2014
Central Concept: Relationships
Related Concepts: Defensiveness, Stereotypes, Relational Stages
Approximate Scene Location: 14 minutes into the 133-minute movie
Approximate Scene Length: 4 minutes
Opening Line: "Hello. . . ."
Closing Line: "I'm not going home with you, so don't even think about it."

Scene Description: Chris (Bradley Cooper) is a Navy SEAL-in-training, having joined the military relatively late (at age 30). During training, he and fellow SEALs are at a bar, and for the first time he sees Taya (Sienna Miller), his future wife, at the bar and walks over to talk to her. Taya seems angry and defensive, and holds strong opinions about SEALs, but Chris is calm and persistent.

Discussion Questions:
1. How does Taya display her anger at SEALs? Do you think her stereotype is fair?
2. What stages of Knapp's relational model do we see?
3. Have you ever held strong opinions about a group of people that were challenged? How were those opinions created? How did being challenged on those opinions change them?

Film: *Boyhood*
Year: 2014
Central Concept: Listening
Related Concept: Relational Messages, Meta-communication
Approximate Scene Location: 34 minutes into the 165-minute movie
Approximate Scene Length: 3 minutes
Opening Line: "You guys ready for the big game?"
Closing Line: "Starting now."

Scene Description: In this scene, the Dad (Ethan Hawke) has picked up Samantha (Lorelei Linklater) and Mason (Ellar Coltrane) for his weekend visit. He is taking them to a ballgame, and he tries to engage them in conversation. After getting only terse replies, he talks about how he'd like to see them communicate, and Mason counters with some thoughts of his own.

Discussion Questions:
1. Do the kids appear to be listening in the initial conversation? What demonstrates that they are or are not listening?
2. What does the dad do to get their attention? Does it work?
3. Mason has a pretty mature response to his dad. Do you think they will be able to adjust how they communicate by discussing it?
4. When have you discussed how you communicate in a relationship? How did the conversation go? Were you able to initiate change?

Film: *Brave*
Year: 2012
Central Concept: Listening
Related Concepts: Listening Styles, Content and Relational Messages, Relational Dialectics
Scene Length and Location: Approximately 2 minutes (Chapter 6: 0:14:00–0:16:10)
Opening Line: "You're muttering."
Closing Line: "Not if I have any say in it."

Scene Description: At some point, many young girls have probably dreamed of being a princess. Not Merida. Instead of wearing beautiful gowns and presiding over her loyal subjects, Merida (voiced by Kelly Macdonald) would rather be riding her horse through the countryside, sharpening her skills with her bow and arrow. Merida's mother, Queen Elinor (voiced by Emma Thompson), has other ideas for her young daughter. In addition to training her to be the next Queen, Elinor also has plans for Merida's romantic relationships: an arranged wedding. In order to set up this scene for analysis, first watch the scene immediately prior (Chapter 5, 0:12:50–0:14:00). There, we learn what sparked the conflict between Merida and her mother.

In this scene for analysis, King Fergus (voiced by Billy Connolly) finds his wife, Elinor, brooding over her conflict with Merida. To help her work through this problem, Fergus suggests that they role-play: he will be Merida, and she can play herself. Despite Elinor's initial reluctance, and Fergus's over-the-top performance, we gain valuable insight into Elinor and Merida's relationship and how they perceive each other. If Elinor and Merida truly want each other to listen, then it will take more than simply hearing the other person speak.

Discussion Questions:
1. Identify the personal listening styles of Merida and Queen Elinor.
2. How can Merida and her mother improve their listening? Which type of listening—informational, critical, or empathic—would you suggest they use for this situation? Why?
3. How does the content of their relational messages influence, and possibly interfere with, Merida and her mother's attempts to understand each other? Identify which relational messages are most influential in their conversations.
4. Which dialectical tensions are Merida and Queen Elinor experiencing? What advice would you give them to better manage these tensions?
5. Think about your own experiences with mother-daughter relationships, either firsthand or through relationships you have witnessed. Is there a singular communication issue that typically defines this relationship? Are there typical differences in listening? Dialectics? Conflict styles? Please explain your answer.

Film: *Clueless*
Year: 1995
Central Concept: Language
Related Concepts: Culture, Communication Competence, Public Speaking
Approximate Scene Location: 30 seconds into the 97-minute film
Approximate Scene Length: 4 minutes
Opening Line: "Did I show you the lumped-out Jeep daddy got me?"
Closing Line: "If she doesn't do the assignment, I can't do mine."

Scene Description: Cher (Alicia Silverstone) and her friends live in their own "contempo-casual" culture and speak their own language (depicted throughout this scene with words such as "jeepin," "outie," and "buggin'"). Their linguistic code gives them a sense of shared identity and excludes those who are not in their group. Near the end of the scene, Cher uses her group's jargon in a public speaking context, and her speech is not successful, demonstrating that language which is appropriate for an informal context is not appropriate for a formal one.

Discussion Questions:
1. Identify words/terms used by Cher and her friends that are unique to their culture. Which words/terms were not familiar to you?
2. Why do teenagers create new words and/or give old words new meanings?
3. Is it appropriate to use slang and jargon in public speeches?
4. Discuss this scene in terms of interpersonal, intercultural, and public speaking competence.

Film: *Crazy, Stupid, Love*
Year: 2011
Central Concept: Listening
Related Concepts: Identity Management, Scripts, Self-Disclosure, Expectancy Violations
Length and Location of Scene: Approximately 3 minutes (Chapter 5: 0:41:32–0:44:02)
Opening Line: "Just no talking about your kids, your job."
Closing Line: "That's what you picked up from what I just said?"

Scene Description: Cal Weaver (Steve Carell) is your stereotypical middle-aged man: married to his wife for twenty-plus years, with three children, a large house, and a steady job. When his wife, Emily (Julianne Moore), unexpectedly reveals that she cheated on him and wants a divorce, Cal's life is turned upside down and inside out. Although he capitulates and moves into an apartment, it's clear that Cal misses his relationship with Emily. To combat his depression and loneliness, Cal begins frequenting the local bar scene. There, he meets Jacob (Ryan Gosling), a self-proclaimed savant when it comes to talking with, and taking home, women. Jacob takes pity on Cal, and vows to teach him "the art of the pick-up."

Prior to this scene Cal has already observed how Jacob interacts with women, successfully administering one pick-up line after another. Now, Jacob convinces Cal that he is ready to "fly solo" and secure a date on his own. Jacob singles out Kate (Marisa Tomei), introductions are made, and the initial interaction ensues. Observe how Cal navigates this uncharted territory, as his identity management and self-disclosure are unique, to put it mildly. And pay close attention to Kate as well. After listening to Cal, is she really going to fall for his advances?

Discussion Questions:
1. Which type of faulty or ineffective listening behavior is Kate guilty of as she listens to Cal? In addition, what are the possible reasons why Kate engages in this type of ineffective listening?
2. Identify a time in your life when you were the one who demonstrated ineffective listening. What effect did your faulty listening have on the conversation? How can you work toward reducing your ineffective listening?

3. In the scene, Cal comments on several things that he "was supposed to say. . . ." In other words, Cal was encouraged to use a conversational script, and in particular a dating script. How common are scripts during initial interactions, and particularly in the dating context? Do you notice these scripts, and if so, what are your reactions when you hear them? Do they work?

4. Looking at this scene from a self-disclosure perspective, and particularly the social penetration model, how would you describe the depth and breadth of information Cal volunteered? Did he follow the typical rules for effective self-disclosure? Explain.

5. How would the expectancy violation model explain the outcome of their conversation? Use the terms *expectancies, violation valence*, and *communicator reward valence* in your answer.

Film: *Dallas Buyers Club*
Year: 2013
Central Concept: Communication Climate
Related Concepts: Perception, Language, Content and Relational Messages, Gender and Sex Roles
Length and Location of Scene #1: 2 minutes, 30 seconds (exact location 0:31:04–0:34:34)
Opening Line: "My name is Rayon."
Closing Line: "Anyone who plays cards like you ain't got five grand anyhow."

Scene Description: In this scene, Ron Woodroof (Matthew McConaughey) first meets the transgendered Rayon (Jared Leto) who is also in the hospital from AIDS-related illness. Although Ron is uncomfortable by Rayon being transgender, the two start playing cards, with Rayon taking Ron's money. Rayon reveals that he's being paid to test AZT for a friend.

Discussion Questions (Scene #1):
1. What perceptual tendencies may have led to troublesome communication in this scene?
2. Identify as many nonverbal cues as you can (e.g., haptics, proxemics, etc.) that are played out in the scene and discuss their relationship to the communication climate.
3. Compare the characters' content messages with their relational messages. Do their relational messages support the content of what they say, or do they contradict?
4. What role did impression management play in how Rayon and Ron communicated with each other?
5. Think about when your perceptions were distorted about someone you learned to care about. Identify what influenced those inaccurate perceptions? Where they distorted perceptions about yourself? How have you learned to be more empathic to others?

Length and Location of Scene #2: 3 minutes (exact location 1:25:25–1:28:25)
Opening Line: "I met someone who's been very kind to me."
Closing Line: "Thank you."

Scene Description: The scene begins with Rayon (Jared Leto) dressed in masculine clothing asking his father for money to help keep the Dallas Buyers Club afloat. A handshake and a hug at the end symbolize Ron Woodroof's (Matthew McConaughey) transformation from a homophobic bigot to a less judgmental version of his former self.

Discussion Questions (Scene #2):

1. Compare Rayon's presenting self in the first scene versus the second scene. What about Rayon's identity management has changed? Use the terms *manner*, *appearance*, and *setting* in your answer.
2. Looking at both of these scenes together, social expectations and our relationships with others have a powerful influence on how we communicate. What does this observation tell you about sex and gender roles?
3. Analyze how Ron and Rayon communicate in this scene (verbal and nonverbal) that demonstrates an improvement in their relationship.
4. Recall a relationship with someone that changed your perceptions, attitudes, and communication positively. Identify what changed.
5. Consider your own experiences managing your identity, gendered or otherwise. Think of a particular moment when you struggled to hide your true self from someone else. Analyze why you were cautious in revealing your identity. Was it fear of being judged? Was it the need to save face, either yours or someone else's? Please explain.

Film: *Dead Man Walking*
Year: 1996
Central Concept: Perception (Stereotyping and Prejudice)
Related Concepts: Communication Climate, Listening, Language
Approximate Scene Location: 40 minutes into the 120-minute film
Approximate Scene Length: 3 minutes
Opening Line: "Rain, rain, rain . . . that's a bad sign." (in the middle of a prison cell discussion)
Closing Line: "Can we talk about something else?"

Scene Description: This scene is an interpersonal communication tour de force. Helen Prejean (Susan Sarandon) is a nun who befriends death-row prisoner Matthew Poncelet (Sean Penn) prior to his execution. She confronts Poncelet about his prejudices regarding African-Americans. Poncelet's perceptions and language are filled with stereotypes and generalizations about "niggers" and "coloreds." Prejean's questions and responses require him to think (which he doesn't seem to want to do) about inaccuracies in his generalizations. Some of her comments are loaded and get defensive reactions; most are reflective and allow Poncelet to hear his prejudices in another voice. When Prejean's probing digs too deep (she gets him to realize "it's lazy people you don't like," not blacks), Poncelet asks Prejean to change the subject—which she agrees to do. This scene is worthy of line-by-line analysis.

Discussion Questions:

1. What factors influenced Poncelet's perceptions, prejudices, and stereotypes?
2. What listening skills does Prejean use to draw information from Poncelet? How do these skills get/keep Poncelet talking and thinking?

3. What questions/statements by Prejean prompt a defensive response from Poncelet?
4. Discuss the use of responsible and irresponsible language in the scene and its relationship to communication climate.

Film: *The Descendants*
Year: 2011
Central Concept: Self-Disclosure
Related Concepts: Privacy, Conflict, Relational Dialectics
Length and Location of Scene: Approximately 5 minutes (Chapter 10: 0:29:35–0:34:15)
Opening Line: "Watch your sister."
Closing Line: "I guess it doesn't matter."

Scene Description: In his own words, Matt King (George Clooney) is "the back-up parent," while his wife Elizabeth (Patricia Hastie) is the one who manages the relationships in their family and takes care of their two daughters. Sadly, Elizabeth was recently involved in a boating accident, and now she lies in a hospital bed in a coma. Because of the accident, Matt is forced to reexamine his life: his workaholic nature, the pending sale of his family's expansive land trust, and what it means to be a loving husband and father. When her doctor diagnoses Elizabeth's condition as terminal, Matt suddenly realizes that he alone will have to break the news to their friends and family members. And when Matt learns that Elizabeth was having an affair before the accident, he's not quite sure what to think.

In this scene, Matt's older daughter Alexandra (Shailene Woodley) has just told him about the affair—which is why she had been so angry with her mother. Stupefied, Matt runs over to the home of Elizabeth's friend, Kai (Mary Birdsong) and her husband Mark (Rub Huebel). There, Matt confronts Kai and Mark about their knowledge of the affair. To label this moment as emotionally awkward would be an understatement. Watch how the characters manage their disclosure of this private information, and their decisions to conceal or reveal. If you were in this situation, what would you do? **Note: Consider pausing the scene about halfway through, at the 0:32:42 mark, and discuss the first two discussion questions that follow. Then watch the remainder of the scene to answer questions 3 and 4.**

Discussion Questions:
1. Place yourself in Kai and Mark's position, one at a time. How would you have handled knowing this private information (the affair) if you were Kai? Would you have disclosed this information to Matt? What if you were Mark? Does gender make a difference?
2. Which dialectical tensions are demonstrated in this scene? How does each of the characters choose to manage these dialectics? Hint: All three characters make different choices.
3. Why did Matt suddenly reveal to Kai that his wife, Elizabeth, is going to die? Was Matt's disclosure appropriate or not? Whose disclosure was more justified: Kai's decision to keep the affair a secret or Matt's decision to disclose Elizabeth's diagnosis at this moment? Please explain your reasoning.
4. What are some criteria or questions that you ask of yourself when you are deciding whether to reveal private information to someone else? Please make a list of these criteria and compare with another classmate. Any similarities? Differences?

Film: *Election*
Year: 1999
Central Concept: Persuasion
Related Concept: Public Speaking
Approximate Scene Location: 36 minutes into the 103-minute film
Approximate Scene Length: 5 minutes
Opening Line: "We'll move on now to the presidential race."
Closing Line: "Don't vote at all!"

Scene Description: Three candidates are running for student government president at Carver High School: Tracy (Reese Witherspoon), Paul (Chris Klein), and Tammy (Jessica Campbell). Each is required to give a brief speech at a student assembly. Tracy's presentation is memorized, well constructed, and delivered with precision and flair (and a dose of overconfidence, which generates crude catcalls from students who think she is stuck up). Paul, a popular athlete, reads his speech directly from his notecards. While his content is solid, he has little or no eye contact, facial expression, or vocal variety—and the students don't know how to respond (they are prompted to applaud by a teacher). Tammy, Paul's sister, thinks that student government is a joke; she is running for election to spite her brother and his girlfriend. She speaks extemporaneously and with passion about the "pathetic" election process and encourages people to either vote for her or not vote at all. She gets a rousing response.

Discussion Questions:
1. Identify the strengths and weaknesses of each of the candidates' speeches.
2. Evaluate the persuasive appeals of each candidate in terms of logos, pathos, and ethos.
3. Which candidate would get your vote—and why?

Film: *Friends with Benefits*
Year: 2011
Central Concept: Intimacy
Related Concepts: Friends with Benefits Relationships, Social Exchange Theory, Relationship Rules, Relational Dialectics
Length and Location of Scene: Approximately 5 minutes (Chapter 5: 0:24:20–0:29:20)
Opening Line: "I can't do this anymore."
Closing Line: "Swear."

Scene Description: Dylan (Justin Timberlake) is an art director at a small Internet company in California, and Jamie (Mila Kunis) is a corporate head hunter based out of New York City. When Jamie successfully recruits Dylan to be the new art design coordinator for *GQ* magazine in New York, she is the only person he knows in the entire city. They soon become platonic friends, as both of them recently ended an intimate relationship, and emotional commitment is currently at the bottom of their respective lists. However, their mutual need for physical intimacy is still rather high. Dylan and Jamie decide to try to maintain their relationship as friends, but with sexual benefits. Can two friends keep their relationship strictly physical—just sex—without any emotional intimacy?

In this scene, Jamie and Dylan are spending time together, as platonic friends, watching romantic movies. As they talk about their past romantic relationships, both of them realize that right now they want a sexual relationship without emotions or commitment. Together they make a pact and decide to give the "friends-with-benefits relationship" a try. Considering what you have learned about the definitions of intimacy and commitment, do Jamie and Dylan have a "real" interpersonal relationship?

Discussion Questions:
1. Use social exchange theory to describe the potential costs and rewards of a friends-with-benefits relationship. Are their possible differences between males' and females' cost/reward analysis of friends-with-benefits relationships?
2. How might male and female intimacy styles affect this type of relationship? Explain.
3. Based on your knowledge of friends-with-benefits relationships, create a list of "rules" that could be used to maintain this type of relationship. How do these maintenance rules differ from platonic cross-sex friendships? From romantic relationships?
4. Which relational dialectics would be most prominent in a friends-with-benefits relationship? How would partners in this type of relationship manage these dialectics?

Film: *Fruitvale Station*
Year: 2013
Central Concept: Emotions
Related Concepts: Conflict, Culture, Intercultural Communication
Length and Location of Scene: 1 minute, 25 seconds (*Interplay* YouTube Channel; exact location 0:24:53–0:26:33)
Opening Line: "I'm not coming here for these visits anymore."
Closing Line: "Hey, Ma. I'm sorry."

Scene Description: In this scene, Oscar Grant III (Michael B. Jordan) is confronted by his mother Wanda (Octavia Spencer) during a prison visit. The conversation starts out lightheartedly, but soon turns to Oscar's child. Wanda pushes Oscar by presenting him with the consequences of his actions on his daughter, which elicits an explosive reaction on his part. **Note: The clip on the YouTube channel has been edited to avoid profanity. Instructors can show the full clip, with profanity, using the times indicated above.**

Discussion Questions:
1. Map the way in which Oscar's intensity of emotions changes throughout the conversation. Which provocations trigger each specific reaction? In other words, what is the activating event?
2. Do ethnicity and cultural background play a role in how both Oscar and Wanda express themselves? Think about tense interactions you've had with your family members, and how emotions were expressed during these situations.
3. Would you characterize Oscar's feelings as facilitative or debilitative emotions? Does this classification have anything to do with intensity? If you classify Oscar's emotions as debilitative, how can he get rid of these negative feelings?
4. If we expand our definition of "culture" beyond the traditional, does this scene depict intercultural communication? Why or why not?

Film: *The Grand Budapest Hotel*
Year: 2014
Central Concept: Perception
Related Concepts: Emotional Expression, Relational Messages, Listening
Approximate Scene Location: 59 minutes into the 99-minute movie
Approximate Scene Length: 4 minutes
Opening Line: "Good evening."
Closing Line: "I insist you finish later."

Scene Description: Gustave (Ralph Fiennes) is the very well-known concierge at the Grand Budapest Hotel. He has been framed for the murder of a wealthy patroness, and has been put in jail. His protégé (and the lobby boy at the Grand Budapest), Mr. Moustafa (F. Murray Abraham), has smuggled tools into the jail so Gustave and a few other convicts can escape. This scene begins with Gustave climbing out of the sewer and meeting up with Moustafa, and then questioning Moustafa's escape plans.

Discussion Questions:
1. What are Gustave's expectations of a great escape from jail? How do they compare to the reality of his situation?
2. Why does Gustave lash out at Moustafa? How does Moustafa react?
3. How do the two men differ in terms of their emotional expression?
4. What expectations have you had in a situation that influenced how you perceived the situation? How did you communicate in that situation? What was the outcome?

Film: *The Great Gatsby*
Year: 2013
Central Concept: Nonverbal Communication
Related Concepts: Identity Management, Relational Messages
Approximate Scene Location: 52 minutes into the 143-minute movie
Approximate Scene Length: 4 minutes
Opening Line: "Is there anything you need?"
Closing Line: "I'm certainly glad to see you as well."

Scene Description: Nick Carroway (Tobey Maguire) moves into a cottage next door to the eccentric millionaire Jay Gatsby (Leonardo DiCaprio). He discovers that Gatsby knew and was in love with his cousin Daisy five years previously. Gatsby asks Nick to invite Daisy to tea so Gatsby can see her again. After sending gardeners over to Nick's cottage to clean up the grounds, Gatsby arrives for tea with an extensive menu of food and a proliferation of flowers. This scene begins with Gatsby nervously waiting for Daisy to arrive and goes through their first interaction in five years.

Discussion Questions:
1. Identify the range of identities Gatsby displays. How is he using his nonverbals to present those identities?
2. Though few words are exchanged between Gatsby and Daisy, it seems much more is communicated. What relational messages are conveyed? How are they conveyed?

3. What are the functions of the nonverbal in this scene?
4. How do you create your identities? What nonverbals do you use to create an identity at school? At work? On a date?

Film: *The Help*
Year: 2011
Central Concept: Listening
Related Concepts: Supportive Listening, Confirmation, Self-Fulfilling Prophecy
Length and Location of Scene: Approximately 3 minutes (Chapter 3: 0:23:15–0:26:00)
Opening Line: "What you doing hiding out here, girl?"
Closing Line: "Come on go home with me until the dance is over. Come on."

Scene Description: Set in Civil Rights-torn Jackson, Mississippi, in the 1960s, *The Help* is a fictional story about Skeeter Phelan (Emma Stone). Always the rebellious one in her family, Skeeter eschews the socialite lifestyle of her friends. After graduating from Ole Miss, she seeks out and earns a job as a journalist. However, writing for the local paper about housekeeping tips is not what Skeeter had in mind. Instead, she hatches the idea of writing a book about the stories of black housekeepers—known as "the help"—who work for well-to-do white families in Jackson. Recruiting the housekeepers turns out to be a challenge, but Skeeter eventually finishes her book. And when it hits the store shelves, it creates quite the scandal in Jackson. On the surface, *The Help* is about people overcoming prejudice and racism in their community. But it's also about listening to people tell their stories. And, to paraphrase a line from the film, it's about confirming that all of us are "kind, smart, and important."

Immediately before this scene, Skeeter has learned that her mother, Charlotte (Allison Janney), recently fired the family's longtime housekeeper, Constantine (Cicely Tyson). Angry and bitter, Skeeter storms out of the house and marches straight toward a sitting bench on the family property. As she gets closer to the bench, Skeeter relives a teenage moment when Constantine comforted her. Watch how Constantine's supportive listening style confirms Skeeter's identity, and sets her back on a path of positive self-regard. **Note: There are several additional scenes of confirmation in the film, particularly when another housekeeper (Aibileen, played by Viola Davis) speaks to the children she watches over.**

Discussion Questions:
1. Describe how Constantine uses supportive listening with Skeeter. Which particular types of supportive responses does Constantine use? Is a combination of responses always effective? Please explain.
2. How does Constantine create a self-fulfilling prophecy for Skeeter? Do you believe Skeeter will internalize this self-fulfilling prophecy? Why or why not?
3. Recall a moment in your life when someone was a supportive listener for you. Specifically, what did the other person say and do to make you feel supported? Please describe in detail.
4. Do you consider yourself to be a good listener? What are specific goals you can set for yourself to be a more supportive listener of others? Please make a list of these goals now, and in one week revisit the list. Were you successful improving your listening skills?

Film: *Her*
Year: 2013
Central Concept: Computer-Mediated Communication/Technology/Social Media
Related Concepts: Self-Disclosure, Identity Management

Scene #1 Length and Location: Approximately 2 minutes and 20 seconds (*Interplay* YouTube channel; exact location 0:60:48–0:63:08)
Opening Line: "I even made a new friend."
Closing Line: "It's kind of like a form of socially acceptable insanity."

Scene Description: In the not-too-distant future, Theodore Twombly (Joaquin Phoenix) lives alone in a high-rise apartment, wounded on the heels of a failed marriage. He spends his days in a cubicle at BeautifulHandwrittenLetters.com writing warm, sensitive messages for other people.

Theodore's life changes when he buys an artificially intelligent operating system who calls herself Samantha (voiced by the disembodied Scarlett Johansson). With a beguiling personality and insights more keen than those of most humans, Samantha draws Theodore out of his self-imposed shell and helps him find joy in everyday life. Before long they grow to love one another. As in every relationship, the couple struggles to meet their differing needs.

Unlike most flesh-and-blood partners, Theodore and Samantha build their relationship entirely on speech. Their only tools are their words and voices. That's enough to achieve a level of intimacy most couples would relish.

It's easy to view this romance as a warning about the dangers of our digital era. Whether or not technology can indeed satisfy our interpersonal needs, the movie *Her* demonstrates that emotional connection is what humans crave, and that they'll go to great lengths to find it.

In this scene, Theodore's friend Amy (Amy Adams) confides in him that she has struck up a friendship with an operating system. In turn, he confesses that he is dating Samantha, and may be falling in love with her. **Note: The clip on the YouTube channel has been edited to exclude the characters' discussion of sex. Instructors can show the full clip using the times indicated above.**

Discussion Questions:
1. Identify the types of technologies you utilize to initiate or maintain relationships. In what ways might your relationships with these technologies themselves be considered intimate?
2. Is mediated communication sometimes preferable to face-to-face interaction? When is this the case, and how so?
3. Consider the self-disclosures in this scene. How are the characters' revelations risky or beneficial?
4. Have you ever made a self-disclosure you were reluctant to make? How did you manage your identity in light of it?

Film: *He's Just Not That Into You*
Year: 2009
Central Concept: Technology
Related Concepts: Computer-Mediated Communication, Relational Stages, Relational Maintenance
Approximate Scene Location: 67 minutes into the 129-minute film
Approximate Scene Length: 2 minutes
Opening Line: "He's leaving his wife for me!"
Closing Line: "Yeah . . . I felt like we connected."

Scene Description: Inspired by a pop culture book with the same name, *He's Just Not That Into You* dispenses romantic advice to its hopelessly confused female cast. Stacked with stereotypes, the entire film is intended to be a lesson on reading subtle verbal and nonverbal cues of potential romantic partners—to determine if he really is "into you." In this scene, Mary (Drew Barrymore) is expressing her frustration with today's technologically driven dating culture. Exasperated, Mary tells her girlfriend Anna (Scarlett Johansson) how she longs for simpler times when technology was less ubiquitous and dating was a face-to-face experience.

Discussion Questions:
1. Explain why Mary is so upset. Does she have a legitimate complaint? Why or why not?
2. Identify the types of technologies (e.g., e-mail, cell phones, social networking sites) you utilize to *initiate* romantic relationships. Which medium is the most effective? Why? Which mediums are more effective for *maintaining* romantic relationships?
3. Describe a personal example when you experienced *benefits* from using technology instead of face-to-face communication. What is gained by using these technologies?
4. Likewise, describe a personal example when you felt *restricted* by using technology instead of face-to-face communication. What is lost by using these technologies?

Film: *Hitch*
Year: 2005
Central Concept: Interpersonal Relationships
Related Concepts: Nonverbal, Gender Influence on Relationships
Approximate Scene Location: 43 minutes into the 118-minute movie
Approximate Scene Length: 9 minutes
Opening Line: "Keep it simple, like we practiced."
Closing Line: "When they're good."

Scene Description: In *Hitch*, Alex "Hitch" Hitchens (Will Smith) is a New York date doctor who teaches men how to romance the women of their dreams. Hitch's latest client is Albert Brennaman (Kevin James), a nerdy financial consultant who needs to develop a more macho communication style to win the heart of wealthy and beautiful Allegra Cole (Amber Valletta). The scene provides many examples of incompetent interactions and dating behaviors to discuss.

Discussion Questions:
1. How, specifically, does Hitch encourage Albert to change his verbal communication when interacting with Allegra?
2. Which nonverbal behaviors does Hitch coach Albert to change, and why?
3. What bits of advice does Hitch offer Albert to increase his attractiveness? Which tips do you believe are and are not sound?

Film: *Hope Springs*
Year: 2012
Central Concept: Relational Maintenance
Related Concepts: Relational Stages, Relational Maintenance Strategies, Relational Dialectics

Scene Length and Location: Approximately 4 minutes (Chapter 1: 0:02:50–0:06:55)
Opening Line: (alarm clock rings in the background)
Closing Line: (Kay and Arnold close their bedroom doors)

Scene Description: Kay (Meryl Streep) and Arnold (Tommy Lee Jones) have been married for 31 years. For Arnold, the length of their relationship is evidence enough of their happiness—Arnold's logic is that if they weren't happy, they wouldn't still be married. Not surprisingly, Kay does not share Arnold's circular reasoning. Kay is unhappy in her marriage, and probably has been for some time. After raising a family and sending her children off into the world, Kay finds herself with "nothing to look forward to." Desperate to save their relationship, Kay wants to attend couples counseling with a marriage therapist (Steve Carell) in Maine. Arnold reluctantly agrees to go along, and he quickly realizes just how serious, and unhappy, Kay is. In the end, can Arnold and Kay truly change their marriage for the better?

In this series of scenes, we observe the current state of Kay and Arnold's marriage. If we were asked to label this relationship, the word "routine" would likely come to mind. Yet, there is hope. If Kay gets her way, she and Arnold will once again have a "real" marriage.

Discussion Questions:
1. Using Knapp's staircase model, identify which relationship stage(s) Kay and Arnold are experiencing. What characteristics of their relationship demonstrate this stage? Please analyze and explain.
2. Toward the beginning of the scene, Kay asks her co-worker if a marriage can be changed. What are your thoughts on this topic? Can partners in a marriage in particular or a romantic relationship in general change their relationship for the better? How does your answer influence your expectations of relationships, even prior to entering one? Could these expectations constitute a self-fulfilling prophecy?
3. Consider the typology of relational maintenance strategies (e.g., positivity, assurances, sharing tasks, etc.). Which ones do Kay and Arnold lack in their relationship? How much do these maintenance strategies influence partners' ability to keep a relationship going?
4. Which relational dialectic is Kay primarily experiencing in her marriage with Arnold? How is she managing this dialectical tension?

5. Although it is not evident in this scene, a recurring theme in the film is the importance of sexual satisfaction in a relationship. From your experience, can sexual satisfaction act as a relational maintenance strategy? How important is sexual compatibility (i.e., frequency, expectations, talking about it, etc.) for partners to experience relational satisfaction?

Film: *The Hunger Games: Catching Fire*
Year: 2013
Central Concept: Conflict
Related Concepts: Ethos/Pathos/Logos, Content and Relational Messages, Power
Length and Location of Scene: Approximately 5 minutes (*Interplay* YouTube channel; exact location 0:17:22–0:22:23)
Opening Line: "The victors of the 74th Hunger Games. . . ."
Closing Line: ". . . and you're going to live happily ever after. You think you can do that?"

Scene Description: In this sequel to *The Hunger Games*, a dystopian tale in which a malevolent government puts adolescent "tributes" in a forested arena where they must fight one another to the death, Katniss Everdeen (Jennifer Lawrence) and Peeta Mellark (Josh Hutcherson) embark on a victors' tour and find themselves targets of the Capitol, as dissent foments in the districts. On the brink of the rebellion and the next Hunger Games, President Snow (Donald Sutherland) announces that this year's tributes will be drawn from among past victors, forcing Katniss and Peeta back into the arena. In this early scene, the pair visits District 11, one of the most impoverished in the country, to honor their fallen tributes.

Discussion Questions:
1. What are the sources of conflict intimated in this scene? What conflict styles do the characters employ?
2. How do Peeta and Katniss utilize appeals to ethos, pathos, and logos? Which type of appeal do you find most persuasive? Why?
3. Compare the characters' content messages with their relational messages. Do their relational messages support the content of what they say, or do they contradict?
4. How are power and powerlessness demonstrated here?

Film: *I Love You, Man*
Year: 2009
Central Concept: Terminating Relationships
Related Concepts: Conflict, Friendship Rules, Relational Maintenance
Approximate Scene Location: 82 minutes into the 105-minute film
Approximate Scene Length: 3 minutes
Opening Line: "Yeah . . . it's open"
Closing Line: "Bye, Anwar."

Scene Description: As the title may suggest, *I Love You, Man* focuses on the male friendship—or "bromance"—between Peter and Sydney. Peter (Paul Rudd) is a newly engaged realtor living in Los Angeles. When his fiancée asks him who his best man will be at their wedding, Peter suddenly realizes that he does not have any male friends. At a chance encounter during a house showing, Peter meets Sydney (Jason Segel), a free-spirited individual also looking for friendship. The remainder of the film follows the stages of Peter and Sydney's relationship, complete with escalating, bonding, and deteriorating. In this scene, Peter confronts Sydney about several recent billboards around Los Angeles baring his likeness. Conflict ensues, Peter and Sydney "break up" and end their friendship. The scene works as an effective illustration of Knapp's terminating stage, along with how individuals establish and violate friendship rules.

Discussion Questions:
1. Explain how this scene demonstrates Knapp's terminating stage of relational deterioration.
2. Are there certain "rules" to follow when ending friendships? Identify three rules you follow.
3. Are there certain "rules" to follow for ending romantic relationships? Identify three rules you follow.
4. Describe a personal example of when you ended a friendship. Was the termination a gradual withdrawal from your friend, or was it a sudden ending of the relationship?
5. In order to avoid reaching the terminating stage, what are strategies you use to maintain a friendship? Identify three relational maintenance strategies you use to keep your friendships from terminating.

Film: *The Invention of Lying*
Year: 2009
Central Concept: Self-Disclosure
Related Concepts: Honesty, Uncertainty Reduction, Identity Management, Saving Face
Approximate Scene Location: 4 minutes into the 99-minute film
Approximate Scene Length: 3 minutes

Opening Line: "This is not as nice as I remember it."
Closing Line: "How is your mom? Alright? Great!"

Scene Description: *The Invention of Lying* is a fictional tale about a world where no one can lie, not even a fib or a white lie—except one man. Mark Bellison (Ricky Gervais) discovers his unique gift and sets out to solve all of the world's problems, become rich and famous, and win the heart of the woman he loves. Predictably, Mark's plans do not always turn out the way he envisioned them. Perhaps the film would be more aptly titled *Too Much Self-Disclosure*, since the storyline really isn't so much about lying. Instead, it's more about the inability to refrain from verbalizing your every thought. The characters say whatever pops into their heads, no matter the context, and apparently without any negative outcomes—indeed a fictional tale. In this scene, Mark is on a date with Anna McDoogles (Jennifer Garner). It is a typical first-date scenario for both characters, complete with feelings of uncertainty and anxiety about each other. Well, it's typical except for one small detail: they cannot control their self-disclosure. Pay special attention to the topics that are discussed, along with their atypical answers. In a world where honesty isn't simply the best policy—it's the only policy—a little self-disclosure can go a very long way.

Discussion Questions:

1. Using the terms *depth*, *breadth*, and *reciprocity of self-disclosure*, how is their first date typical of most first dates? How is it different from most first dates?
2. Consider your own past experiences on first dates. What topics do you typically discuss? Are these topics goal-oriented (e.g., to reduce uncertainty, to secure a second date, etc.)? In what ways?
3. Compare and contrast the characters' public and private selves. How are they managing their identity through communication?
4. Describe a situation in which you were aware of your different selves, and you felt the need to manage your identity. Were you successful?
5. Is honesty always the best policy? Describe a situation in which saving someone's face, without being completely honest, was the best choice—the choice of a competent communicator.

Film: *Invictus*
Year: 2009
Central Concept: Persuasive Speaking
Related Concepts: Credibility, Audience Analysis, Leadership and Power
Approximate Scene Location: 27 minutes into the 134-minute film
Approximate Scene Length: 8 minutes
Opening Line: "And now for the next item on our agenda."
Closing Line: "A luxury. We only needed one more yes than no."

Scene Description: *Invictus* is the real-life story about then South African President Nelson Mandela and his plan to use rugby to unite his country following the demise of apartheid. Set in 1994–1995, newly elected President Mandela (played by Morgan Freeman) is struggling to move his nation forward, both politically and economically, in the eyes of the world. While attending a rugby match of the Springboks, the country's national rugby team, Mandela notices that blacks actually cheer against their home team—for them a longstanding symbol of racism and hatred— while Afrikaners (whites) root for the Springboks. Knowing that South Africa will host the Rugby World Cup in one year, Mandela enlists the aid of the Springboks' captain to promote the sport as a symbol of unity and nationalism instead of hatred and violence. In this scene, Mandela must persuade South Africa's National Sports Council (the governing body in charge of the country's sports) not to change the Springboks team's name and colors. The National Sports Council, like most of the country's black citizens, views the Springboks as a symbol of apartheid. Learning that the Council has voted to dismantle the Springboks, Mandela rushes to their meeting in an attempt to persuade them otherwise. Facing a hostile audience, Mandela uses his credibility and audience analysis to successfully, by a narrow margin, convince the Council of his viewpoint.

Discussion Questions:

1. Using the terms propositions, outcomes, and directness, identify the type of persuasive speech Mandela gives.
2. How does Mandela adapt to his audience (the National Sports Council)? What strategies does he use to appeal to this target audience?

3. Recall a time when you gave a speech to persuade, even an informal talk to a group. What strategies did you use to adapt to your audience? Were you successful? If not, how could you have increased your success through improved audience analysis?
4. Consider Mandela's credibility as a speaker. What characteristics about him increase the audience's perception of his credibility? How does Mandela use these characteristics in his speech?
5. Think back to a moment when you were in the audience for a persuasive speech. Did you consider the speaker to be credible? Why? If not, what could the speaker have done to increase your perceptions of his or her credibility?
6. Identify the types of power Mandela uses to influence the National Sports Council. How are power and credibility necessarily interwoven? Is it possible to separate them?

Film: *The Iron Lady*
Year: 2011
Central Concept: Public Speaking
Related Concepts: Speaker Credibility, Delivery
Length and Location of Scene: Approximately 4 minutes (Chapter 7: 0:40:35–0:44:05)
Opening Line: "What is it you took away from your visit, which may be of value here in Great Britain?"
Closing Line: "They are absolutely non-negotiable."

Scene Description: In *The Iron Lady* Meryl Streep is a tour de force as Margaret Thatcher, the embattled first female Prime Minister of Great Britain. Politics aside, Streep gives a remarkable performance as she demonstrates the challenges that Thatcher experienced, especially as a female leader. Much of the film portrays Thatcher in her later years as a forgetful scion of the old guard who frequently has conversations with her deceased husband. However, interspersed throughout the film are scenes of Thatcher's rise to power and authority. And within those scenes are excellent examples of public speaking, speaker credibility, and leadership.

In this scene, Thatcher is only considering running for the opposing party of Great Britain's Parliament—becoming Prime Minister has not yet crossed her mind. After her two political consultants intently watch an interview that Thatcher gave, they are none too shy about critiquing her performance. They offer advice to improve her credibility and make her resemble a leader with "more importance." Thatcher takes the criticism in stride, offering her own opinion on how the audience sees her. Do you agree with her consultants' advice, or should Thatcher ultimately "just be herself"? **Note: If you allow the film to run past this scene, we are shown Thatcher receiving voice lessons—a friendly reminder that even polished public speakers need practice.**

Discussion Questions:
1. In your opinion, do you agree that Margaret Thatcher needed to "change her voice" and "get rid of those hats"? Why or why not? How might these qualities influence judgments of her competence, character, and charisma?
2. Concerning the credibility of a speaker, how influential is one's voice to persuade an audience? What about one's appearance? Which particular aspect of delivery (voice,

gestures, eye contact, or appearance) is most important for capturing the attention of an audience, and ultimately persuading them?

3. Are the challenges of persuasion different for male and female speakers? How does the context or occasion of the speech influence these challenges? What about the topic of the speech?

4. Recall a speech that you gave to an audience, or a speaker that you witnessed, and analyze the credibility of the speaker (you or someone else). What did you (or the speaker) do to enhance your (or their) credibility in the minds of the audience? Were these strategies successful? Why or why not?

Film: *The Joy Luck Club*
Year: 1993
Central Concept: Culture
Related Concept: Communication Competence
Approximate Scene Location: 43 minutes into the 138-minute film
Approximate Scene Length: 4 minutes
Opening Line: "The next week I brought Rich to Mom's birthday dinner." (Waverly's voice)
Closing Line: "All this needs is a little soy sauce."

Scene Description: Waverly, a Chinese-American woman (Tamlyn Tomita), brings her Anglo-American boyfriend Rich (Christopher Rich) home for a dinner cooked by her Chinese mother, Lindo (Tsai Chin). Rich unknowingly insults Waverly's family when he fails to follow the rules of Chinese dining. For instance, he shocks everyone at the table by taking a large first serving of the entree. As Waverly explains in her narration, it is customary in Chinese culture to take only a small spoonful of a dish until everyone else has had some. Rich's biggest mistake is when he misunderstands Lindo's description of her prized entree. Lindo says, "This dish no good. Too salty." Rich decodes the message literally, not paying attention to Lindo's nonverbal cues. The family knows that when Lindo insults her cooking, it means she is pleased with it. The implicit rule is to eat some, then compliment it profusely. Instead, Rich floods the prized dish with soy sauce and assures Lindo that it is not beyond repair.

Discussion Questions:
1. What differences between American and Chinese cultures are depicted in this scene? Use terms from the lecture and text in your analysis.
2. What could Rich have done to enhance his intercultural competence?

Film: *The King's Speech*
Year: 2010
Central Concept: Public Speaking
Related Concepts: Stage Fright, Delivery, Articulation
Length and Location of Scene: Approximately 4 minutes (exact location 0:34:25–0:38:40)
Opening Line: "Strictly business. No personal nonsense."
Closing Line: "Father."

Scene Description: Colin Firth is Prince Albert (or "Bertie" to his family), the second in line to the throne of England and a man with a bit of a speaking problem. Although Bertie dreads the thought of becoming king and giving public speeches, he accepts the position when his older brother, David, abdicates. Bertie's wife, Queen Elizabeth (Helena Bonham Carter), witnesses her husband struggling to keep his confidence and the public's trust, so she enlists the help of speech therapist Lionel Logue (Geoffrey Rush).

This series of scenes shows Lionel training Bertie in the art of public speaking. Although his methods are unusual, Lionel seems to be making progress with the reluctant King. The audience can only hope that Lionel's unorthodox techniques will cure the King of his "bloody stammer" and instill the poise he needs to lead England.

Discussion Questions:
1. What is your opinion of Lionel's strategies to help the King? Do you believe these strategies would really be effective in reducing his stage fright? Why or why not?
2. How common is stage fright for the average person who is about to give a speech? Do you know anyone, either famous or otherwise, who experiences stage fright?
3. What techniques do you use to manage your own stage fright before, and even during, a public speech? How successful have you been with these techniques?
4. Analyze your own delivery skills. Which parts of your delivery give you confidence? Which parts would you like to improve?

Film: *Lincoln*
Year: 2012
Central Concept: Public Speaking
Related Concepts: Persuasion, Narrative Style, Ethos/Pathos/Logos, Delivery

Scene Length and Location: Approximately 7 minutes (Chapter 4: 0:23:20–0:30:50)
Opening Line: "Thunder forth, God of War."
Closing Line: "And come February the first, I intend to sign the Thirteenth Amendment!"

Scene Description: In this stirring and critically acclaimed film about Abraham Lincoln (Daniel Day-Lewis), Director Steven Spielberg recounts the president's challenges leading up to the passage of the Thirteenth Amendment to abolish slavery. The film takes an intimate look at Lincoln, peeling back the tableau of his fabled presidency to reveal a man deeply devoted to his family, to his country, and to his morals. Passing the Thirteenth Amendment to the Constitution was no easy task. Indeed, history tells us that Lincoln had to use every persuasive tactic at his disposal to convince—some might say bribe, cajole, and harass—his fellow politicians to support the bill. While history recognizes President Lincoln as a great public orator, the film also illustrates his formidable rhetorical skills in smaller groups, interpersonally and one-on-one. Imagine if the freedom of an entire race were resting on your shoulders. Would you have the communication skills to persuade your audience?

Although it is not one of Abraham Lincoln's traditional public speeches (i.e., one person speaking to many people), this scene illustrates the various tactics he used to persuade others. Pay close attention to the structure of Lincoln's talk, and the reactions of his audience. Likewise, notice how he effectively weaves together ethical, emotional, and logical forms of proof. Not only is this scene an example of persuasive rhetoric, it is also a helpful lesson in American history.

Discussion Questions:
1. What effect does Lincoln's use of narrative (i.e., the opening story) have on his audience? Is his speech more or less persuasive because of the narrative structure?
2. Recall an occasion when you listened to a speaker tell a story as part of the speech. What effect did the story have on you? Can narratives and stories be used ineffectively in public speaking? How so?
3. Does President Lincoln use humor effectively in his speech? Why or why not?
4. Have you ever attempted to use humor in one of your speeches? How effective was it in gaining the attention of your audience? What about persuading your audience?
5. Use Aristotle's three forms of proof (ethos, pathos, and logos) to analyze Lincoln's speech. Which form of proof seems to stand out the most? Was it effective? Why?
6. What aspects of Lincoln's delivery influence the outcome of his speech? Please explain.

Film: *Mean Girls*
Year: 2004
Central Concept: Communication Climate
Related Concepts: Conflict, Empathy
Approximate Scene Location: 70 minutes into the 96-minute film
Approximate Scene Length: 5 minutes, 30 seconds
Opening Line: "Ms. Norbury, you're a successful, caring, intelligent, graceful young woman."
Closing Line: "Suck on that. Aye yie yie yie!" (as she falls backward to be caught by the other girls)

Scene Description: The girls of the junior class at North Shore High School are constantly in conflict. The disagreements, disconfirmation, and backstabbing (including mean evaluations written in a scrapbook called a "Burn Book") reach a breaking point when the fighting nearly leads to a riot. In response, the school principal calls all the junior girls to the gym where one of the school's teachers, Ms. Norbury (Tina Fey), leads them in an "attitude makeover."

Discussion Questions:
1. What is Ms. Norbury's purpose with the two exercises she does where the girls close their eyes? How does it enhance the communication climate and empathy level among the girls?
2. Ms. Norbury says, "You all have got to stop calling each other sluts and whores. It just makes it okay for guys to call you sluts and whores." Do you agree with her assessment? Discuss in terms of course concepts.
3. What style(s) of conflict management does Ms. Norbury use? Is the approach effective in this situation? Discuss how well this approach would (or wouldn't) work in other conflict situations.

Film: *The Perks of Being a Wallflower*
Year: 2012
Central Concept: Communication Competence
Related Concepts: Emotional Expression, Honesty, Self-Disclosure, Relational Dialectics

Scene Length and Location: Approximately 4 minutes (Chapter 14: 1:03:10–1:07:13)
Opening Line: "Things are a total disaster."
Closing Line: "What the hell is wrong with you?"

Scene Description: In this coming-of-age film based on a book of the same name, Charlie (Logan Lerman) has always struggled to fit in. Painfully shy and introverted since he was a little boy, Charlie is now a freshman in high school—an easy target for bullies. Fortunately for him, two seniors (Patrick [Ezra Miller] and Sam [Emma Watson]) take Charlie under their wing and educate him on the finer principles of high school social life. As Charlie expands his horizons—forming lasting friendships, going to parties, and even experiencing his first kiss—his identity slowly becomes more transparent and engaging. Still, Charlie is troubled by his past. He keeps a dark secret buried deep in his psyche, a secret so unfathomable that his mind has hidden it from himself. When Charlie is finally able to comprehend what happened to him, he needs complete support from his family and his first real friends: Patrick and Sam.

In this two-part scene Charlie has started dating Mary Elizabeth (Mae Whitman), a mutual friend of Patrick and Sam. To say that Charlie feels suffocated and controlled by Mary Elizabeth would be an understatement. In the first half of this scene, witness as Charlie pretends to be happy in their relationship. As Charlie is new to the rules of dating, he does not know how to end the relationship—he doesn't even realize that breaking up is an option. In the second part of the scene, Charlie's inexperience and lack of emotional intelligence become quite obvious. Will his friends forgive him for his brutally honest self-disclosure?

Discussion Questions:
1. **Watch the scene up until 1:05:15 and pause it.** How would you describe the relationship between Charlie and Mary Elizabeth? Which relational dialectics are causing tension for Charlie? How is he managing this tension?
2. Is their relationship symmetrical or complementary? Have you ever seen, or perhaps experienced, a relationship like theirs? Did both parties experience relational satisfaction? Please explain.
3. You might argue that Charlie is committing the fallacy of approval: the irrational behavior of seeking everyone else's approval, even to the point of sacrificing one's own happiness. Speculate and analyze why someone might experience this fallacy.
4. **Continue watching the remainder of the scene.** How would you describe Charlie's emotional intelligence? Was his expression of honesty justified? Please explain.
5. If you were Charlie's friend, what advice would you give him about appropriate self-disclosure, emotional expression, and dating?

Film: *Pitch Perfect*
Year: 2012
Central Concept: Perception
Related Concepts: Perception Process, Stereotyping, Culture, Identity

Length and Location of Scene: Approximately 5 minutes (Chapter 2: 0:08:50–0:14:15)
Opening Line: "That's a double-negative."
Closing Line: "What are we going to do?"

Scene Description: *Pitch Perfect* is *Mean Girls* meets *Glee*, with a dash of *Best in Show* sprinkled on top—only with human performers, not dogs. Becca (Anna Kendrick) is the new kid on campus, searching for an identity and a reason to be in college. It doesn't help that her overly protective father is a professor at the same school, or that her new roommate is more than slightly intimidating. Indeed, Becca would rather be anywhere but here. With her talent for mixing musical genres, Becca aspires to be a music producer, not a college freshman. Much to own her surprise, Becca auditions for an all-female a cappella group on campus: the Barden Bellas. The Bellas, after a disastrous performance last year, have their own reputation to salvage. Can Becca's mastery of musical mashups catapult the Bellas to singing success, or is this misfit collection of performers destined to fall flat?

This scene finds Becca, and other characters, wandering around the college's Activities Faire. As the name suggests, the Activities Faire is a showcase of different clubs, groups, and organizations on campus. And as one might expect, each group has its own unique . . . well, let's just say that each group is different. Observe the characteristics of these groups, how they are seen and how they see themselves, and how this influences their communication.

Discussion Questions:
1. How does the perception process (selection, organization, and interpretation) influence the characters' communication with each other?
2. In what ways do the characters engage in stereotyping? What is the basis for these group stereotypes?
3. How does each group demonstrate its own unique culture?
4. Think about the school clubs you belong to now, those you belonged to in high school, or those clubs you knew about. What were the perceptions of these clubs? Why? How did those perceptions influence the ways members were treated by people outside the club?
5. How did being part of a group—an official club or even a social group—influence your identity? Did you find yourself taking on the qualities of the group? How so?

Film: *Precious*
Year: 2009
Central Concept: Self-Disclosure
Related Concepts: Emotional Expression, Ego-boosting, Listening
Approximate Scene Location: 83 minutes into the 109-minute movie
Approximate Scene Length: 3 minutes
Opening Line: "Come with me."
Closing Line: "Write."

Scene Description: Precious (Gabourey Sidibe) is a 16-year-old who has suffered abuse at the hands of both of her parents. By this scene, Precious has given birth to a second child by her father, a product of repeated rape. After her mother turns her abuse to the baby, Precious finally leaves. Precious has been attending an alternative school where her class has become her family, and she is finally learning to read and write. In this scene, Precious is unable to write in her journal, a regular and welcome assignment, and is pushed to disclose what is bothering her, and receives affirmation from her teacher.

Discussion Questions:
1. What prompts Precious to self-disclose? What was the effect of her self-disclosure?
2. Precious gives examples of what she thinks are supposed to be "love"; how might she have gotten to the point where she thinks of these as examples of love?
3. What effect do you think Ms. Rain's affirmation toward Precious might have on her self-esteem? How might it affect her future relationship with her son?

Film: *P.S. I Love You*
Year: 2007
Central Concept: Conflict
Related Concepts: Gender, Punctuation, Content and Relational Messages, Metacommunication, Relational Dialectics
Approximate Scene Location: Opening scene
Approximate Scene Length: 6 minutes
Opening Line: Holly and Gerry are shown walking up steps leaving the subway.
Closing Line: "Kiss mine . . . in English!"

Scene Description: Holly and Gerry are two young people passionately in love with each other. In fact, quite often their passion boils over into a heated argument. This scene begins with Gerry (Gerard Butler) knowing that Holly (Hilary Swank) is angry with him, but not knowing exactly why—her nonverbal communication speaks for itself. As he questions her about the source of this conflict, additional issues about their relationship start to seep out. Gerry becomes frustrated with Holly's insistence that what he says and what he means are two different things, and Holly is equally irritated with Gerry's cavalier approach to their relationship. The scene works on several levels, and mostly because it taps into many students' notions about romantic conflict.

Discussion Questions:
1. What styles of conflict do Holly and Gerry express in this scene? How might their gender differences influence these styles?
2. Holly and Gerry seem to have different perceptions of punctuation, when this conflict really started, and by whom. How is Holly punctuating their argument? Gerry?
3. Explain how the scene illustrates the content and relational dimensions of messages, and identify examples of metacommunication.
4. Which dialectical tension is Holly experiencing, concerning her job and having a baby? How is she choosing to manage this tension? What is Gerry's response?
5. What could Holly and Gerry do to manage this conflict, and future ones, more competently?

Film: *The Pursuit of Happyness*
Year: 2006
Central Concept: Self-Fulfilling Prophecy
Related Concepts: Self-Actualization, Emotional Intelligence
Approximate Scene Location: 107 minutes into the 117-minute movie
Approximate Scene Length: 4 minutes
Opening Line: "Chris, thank you very much."
Closing Line: "Christopher, come here."

Scene Description: Struggling salesman Chris Gardner (Will Smith) pursues a life-changing professional endeavor of becoming a stockbroker under the tremendous pressures of homelessness, tax seizure, jail time, and single parenthood. While caring for his son without any outside help, Gardner endures a grueling unpaid internship. He is determined to win employment in a program where only one of the twenty interns receives a job offer. In this powerful scene, Gardner interacts with his mentor at the end of his internship, when a hiring decision is being made by the company.

Discussion Questions:
1. Describe how Gardner communicates competently with his client and colleagues.
2. Apply the term *self-fulfilling prophecy* to Gardner's life story.
3. How does the final scene exemplify a moment of self-actualization for Gardner?
4. Given the extreme pressures placed on him, explain Gardner's apparent emotional intelligence.

Film: *Selma*
Year: 2014
Central Concept: Relational Messages
Related Concept: Language
Approximate Scene Location: 9 minutes into the 128-minute movie
Approximate Scene Length: 4.5 minutes
Opening Line: "Mr. President, Dr. King."
Closing Line: "Yes, Mr. President, I understand."

Scene Description: In this scene, Dr. Martin Luther King, Jr. (played by David Oyelowo) is meeting with President Johnson (played by Tom Wilkinson), discussing the civil rights movement. The President expresses verbally a desire to help, and Dr. King has a very clear description as to what should happen next. While appearing to be amenable to further progress, President Johnson tries to change the subject, and tries to put off the topic of voting. While Dr. King is respectful of the office of the President, he is direct in his observations, and doesn't allow the subject of voting rights to be dropped.

Discussion Questions:

1. What relational messages are being sent by the nonverbal in this scene? What can we interpret about how these two men feel about each other?
2. The President and Dr. King have different goals in this scene. How do they each use their language to achieve their goals? Which do you think was more effective?
3. Discuss a situation in which you had a goal to accomplish, but you were communicating with someone who had a competing goal they were trying to accomplish. How did you try to achieve your goal? How did you react when the other person was trying to achieve their goal?

Film: *The Social Network*
Year: 2010
Central Concept: Social Media and Communication Competence
Related Concepts: Communication Channels, Emotions, Relational Quality, Conflict
Length and Location of Scene: 1 minute, 08 seconds (YouTube Channel; exact location 0:52:20–0:53:28)
Opening Line: "Could I talk to you alone for a second?"
Closing Line: "Good luck with your video game."

Scene Description: Facebook creator Mark Zuckerberg (Jesse Eisenberg) demonstrates that while he may be a genius at computer programming and meeting the needs of the marketplace, he is a disaster in the domain of personal relationships. In this scene, Erica Albright (Rooney Mara) confronts Mark about how poorly he treated her and the dangers of using the Internet to communicate his views.

Discussion Questions:

1. When Erica told Mark that the Internet isn't written in pencil but in ink, how well do you think he understood the permanent nature of the medium that, ironically, has brought him so much success?
2. Do you agree with Erica that we choose technology to express our negative emotions over other channels more often today?
3. Describe the balance between using face-to-face and social media to communicate in your relationships with others. After assessing the advantages and drawbacks, could that balance be shifted to improve how completely you communicate with someone? How?
4. Analyze an example of using social media from your own life that wasn't communicated competently. What role did the medium play? How could you have communicated your message competently?

Film: *Superbad*
Year: 2007
Central Concept: Communication Competence
Related Concepts: Empathy, Cognitive Complexity, Language
Approximate Scene Location: 11 minutes into the 114-minute film
Approximate Scene Length: 1 minute

Opening Line: "Ms. Hayworth, I joined this class because I thought I would be cooking with a partner."
Closing Line: "Jules."

Scene Description: Seth and his best friend, Evan, are high school seniors desperately searching for one final party before graduation. Most of the time Seth's heart is in the right place, even if his foot is occasionally stuck in his mouth. In this scene, Seth (Johah Hill) attempts to explain to his Home Economics teacher the injustice of not having a cooking partner. During his argument, his language is sprinkled with vulgarity, and he insults his teacher's course, profession, and gender. While Seth does employ a few reasonable strategies to gain her compliance (qualifying his language, apologizing, and initiating subtle touch), his communication incompetence speaks for itself. (Warning: this scene contains some coarse language.)

Discussion Questions:
1. In what ways does Seth exhibit communication incompetence?
2. Consider the three dimensions of empathy. Describe Seth's success rate for each dimension.
3. Would you evaluate Seth as having high cognitive complexity? Why or why not?
4. Seth frequently uses the phrase "no offense" during his talk with Ms. Hayworth. What type of language device is this? Evaluate its effectiveness in this scene compared to your own use of this phrase.

Film: *Thank You for Smoking*
Year: 2006
Central Concept: Persuasion
Related Concepts: Ethos/Pathos/Logos, Social Judgment Theory, Fallacies of Reasoning, Ethics
Approximate Scene Location: 45 minutes into the 92-minute film
Approximate Scene Length: 5 minutes
Opening Line: "Pearl, we got company."
Closing Line: "No, Lorne. Either you keep all the money, or you give it all away."

Scene Description: Based on the novel by Christopher Buckley, this film is a satirical look at both the tobacco industry and the congressional lobbying system. Nick Naylor (Aaron Eckhart) is the Vice President and lead spokesperson for the Academy of Tobacco Studies, an oxymoronic institution if there ever were one. Nick's job—at which he is quite successful—is to persuade whoever is listening that smoking cigarettes is not unhealthy. The film illustrates a variety of fallacious and morally questionable persuasive strategies. In this scene, Nick has been dispatched by big tobacco to the home of the actor who portrayed the Marlboro Man in cigarette ads. Now the actor is dying of lung cancer, and Nick is there to bribe him to keep quiet. What ensues is a clever example of illogical reasoning and unethical persuasion.

Discussion Questions:
1. Provide examples of ethos, pathos, and logos appeals made by Nick in his conversation with the Marlboro Man.
2. Use social judgment theory to explain how Nick successfully persuades the Marlboro Man to take the bribe. Given his high ego-involvement, plot out the Marlboro Man's latitudes of acceptance, rejection, and non-commitment, and arrange Nick's arguments along that continuum.
3. Describe three fallacies of reasoning that Nick uses in his argument. Why did the Marlboro Man not see these fallacies? Which fallacies have you found to be used most often in real-world examples, based on your personal observations?
4. In Nick's own words, his job requires "a moral flexibility" that most people don't have; in other words, it's unethical. Discuss additional, real-world examples of persuasion that you have found to be unethical.

Film: *Trust*
Year: 2010
Central Concept: Self-Disclosure
Related Concepts: Privacy Management, Family Communication, Communication Climate
Length and Location of Scene: Approximately 3 minutes (Chapter 9: 1:15:30–1:18:44)
Opening Line: "Kids! Hurry up, the food's going to be cold."
Closing Line: "Let me go!"

Scene Description: *Trust* is the sobering account of one family's struggle to remain intact following the rape of their daughter, Annie (Liana Liberato). The film begins with a series of fairly innocuous and seemingly harmless scenes of text messages between fourteen-year-old Annie and her cyber-friend, Charlie. Initially Annie and Charlie meet in a chat room about sports. Over the course of several months, and hundreds of texts, they become very close to one another—in fact, Annie develops a crush on Charlie entirely through text messages. Charlie first claims that he is sixteen years old; later on he changes his story to twenty, and finally he says he is twenty-five years old. Despite having been lied to, Annie agrees to meet Charlie in a public place, where she discovers that his age is actually closer to thirty-five. In a disturbing scene Charlie seduces and rapes Annie in his hotel room. The rest of the film wrestles with the aftermath of this crime, including the effects on Annie, her friends, and her family.

In a scene prior to this one, Annie explicitly demanded that her father (Will, played by Clive Owen) not tell her brother (Peter, played by Spencer Curnutt) about what happened to her; Peter has been away at college during the incident. Here, Annie and her family are gathered around the dinner table, discussing their plans and costumes for Halloween. Almost immediately Annie notices that her family is speaking to her in an unexpected manner, and she soon realizes that everyone else knows about what happened to her. Annie confronts her father about violating her privacy, setting off a chain reaction of broken trust, hurt feelings, and conflict. **Note: Additional scenes from this film can also be used to illustrate privacy and self-disclosure as well, especially scenes with Annie, her therapist, and her parents.**

Discussion Questions:

1. Describe the communication climate of this scene, from the beginning to the end, and identify examples of confirming and disconfirming messages directed toward Annie. How does Annie perceive these messages? Confirming? Disconfirming? Why?

2. As the owner of this private information, does Annie have a right to keep her disclosures private from other family members? Why or why not? Did her father violate Annie's privacy, or can his revealing of her disclosure be justified?

3. Recall a moment in your life when you felt that your private disclosure was violated. Was your disclosure revealed intentionally or accidentally? Did you establish any rules with the recipient prior to your disclosure? What did you learn from the experience?

4. What is this particular scene mostly about: self-disclosure, privacy, or communication climate? Please explain and justify your answer with examples.

SECTION II
TELEVISION PROGRAMS

Each of the television programs in this section provides information in the following categories:

TV Show Data: Year, Number of Seasons, Creator(s), Genre, and Episode Length
Characters/Actors: Principal actors and roles in the program
Communication Concepts: Primary communication topics in the program (listed alphabetically)
TV Show Storyline: General background and potential warning information about the television program, as well as a brief summary of its plot and themes.
Discussion Questions: Questions (and answers to the first two) linking the film to communication concepts

The following are a number of television programs that have human communication as a central theme. The discussion questions that follow the basic data about the program are the heart of this section. The questions posed are not the only ones that can or should be asked, nor is there only one "right" way to respond to the questions. In fact, you may argue with some of the analyses and interpretations. That's fine—any good discussion about television programs should engender disagreement. The questions are provided simply to offer an example of how to analyze the program and the communication that goes on within it.

THE BIG BANG THEORY

TV Show Data	
Year Began	2007
Number of Seasons	9
Creator(s)	Chuck Lorre, Bill Prady
Genre	Situation Comedy
Episode Length	30 minutes

Main Cast	
Character	**Actor**
Leonard Hofstadter	Johnny Galecki
Sheldon Cooper	Jim Parsons
Penny	Kaley Cuoco
Howard Wolowitz	Simon Helberg
Raj Koothrappali	Kunal Nayyar
Bernadette Rostenkowski	Melissa Rauch
Amy Farrah Fowler	Mayim Bialik
Stuart Bloom	Kevin Sussman

TV Show Storyline

Described as a TV show "like *Friends* but for nerds," *The Big Bang Theory* is a 30-minute sitcom that began in 2007. The show revolves around the lives of four extremely intelligent, and socially awkward, scientists who work at Caltech University. Leonard and Sheldon, both physicists, are roommates, while Raj (an astrophysicist) and Howard (an aerospace engineer) are their friends and colleagues. The theme of the show explores the general geekiness of the characters, including their poor interpersonal skills, their disturbingly strong penchant for quoting Star Trek, and their shared belief that science can solve any problem. Across the hall from Leonard and Sheldon lives Penny, an aspiring actress who currently waitresses to make ends meet. With her street smarts and advanced social skills, Penny is the perfect foil for the four men. In fact, Penny intrigues Leonard so much that they start dating and develop a romantic relationship. The other two recurring characters, Bernadette and Amy, also work at Caltech, and they become romantically involved with Howard and Sheldon, respectively.

Season 6, Episode 6: "The Extract Obliteration"

Unrelated to the title of this episode, the scene for analysis involves Leonard and Sheldon. Recently, Penny revealed to Leonard that she enrolled in a history course at the local community college. And despite her concern that Leonard would "make a big deal" about it, she tells him that she wrote a paper for the class. When Leonard secretly reads Penny's paper—even though he promised he wouldn't—he needs advice about what to do next. Obviously desperate, Leonard asks Sheldon for help. However, Sheldon has his own interpersonal dilemma: his new online friend, astrophysicist Stephen Hawking, has not been in contact for days. Needless to say, Sheldon has some difficulty being an active listener for Leonard.

Central Concept: Listening
Related Concept: Perception Checking

Scene Length and Location: Exactly 3 minutes (0:10:50–0:13:50)
Opening Line: "Play. Play. Play."
Closing Line: "Oh, of course, it only works on the weak-minded."

Discussion Questions:
1. Identify and describe Leonard's listening style compared to Sheldon's. Are both of their listening responses competent? Why or why not?
2. What do you think about Leonard's solution to use a chess clock? Would the clock encourage active or pseudo listening? Please explain.
3. Leonard outlines two rules of their conversation: they take turns, and each turn includes a response from the friend. How similar are Leonard's rules to the process of perception checking? Compare and contrast the scene with what you have learned about perception checking.
4. When have you encountered poor listeners in your own experiences? Are there certain situations or contexts that discourage active listening? Are certain people simply better listeners than others?

Season 6, Episode 17: "The Monster Isolation"

The scene for analysis in this episode once again illustrates Sheldon's incompetent communication. We see Sheldon recording an online video in what appears to be a long-running series about flags—yes, flags. Their history, their colors, even alternate uses for them—Sheldon discusses all of these topics on "Fun with Flags." To help illustrate how to spark a conversation about flags, Sheldon employs Penny's assistance. However, Penny notices that Sheldon's nonverbal cues are a bit rigid and she gives him some tips about "how to be more open in front of the camera." Naturally, Sheldon takes her advice a bit too far.

Central Concept: Nonverbal Communication

Scene Length and Location: Approximately 3 minutes (0:02:20–0:05:35)
Opening Line: "Hello. I am Dr. Sheldon Cooper."
Closing Line: "Spread your legs; invite them in."

Discussion Questions
1. Identify the different types of nonverbal communication shown in this scene.
2. Which functions of nonverbal communication does Sheldon demonstrate? What meanings would most people attach to Sheldon's nonverbal cues?
3. Like Sheldon, even competent communicators sometimes misinterpret nonverbal cues. Think of a moment in your life when you had difficulty with nonverbal communication, either as the sender or the receiver. What happened? Why did miscommunication occur?

Season 6, Episode 18: "The Contractual Obligation Implementation"

In this episode, Raj is experiencing some serious dating problems—his most recent date, Lucy, snuck away by climbing out of a bathroom window! It seems that Lucy suffers from social anxiety disorder, and going out on dates is a bit of a challenge for her. Undaunted, Raj continues to pursue Lucy and she finally agrees to another date. This time Raj has a plan to make the date less stressful for Lucy: it is a texting date and she will not have to talk to Raj in order to communicate. Ironically, Raj's creative solution might be an unfortunate reality for many daters today.

Central Concept: Technology
Related Concepts: Computer-Mediated Communication

Scene One Length and Location: Approximately 1 minute (0:09:40–0:10:55)
Opening Line: "Excuse me, I'm meeting a girl here."
Closing Line: "I have an adorable accent."

Discussion Questions
1. Although creative, Raj's solution to managing Lucy's dating anxiety is not entirely unprecedented. Describe how you use technology (e.g., texting) before, during, and after a date. Is texting the preferred mode of communication to arrange a date?
2. If you have ever been in a long-distance relationship, or know someone who has, then it's likely that you have seen the pros and cons of using technology to maintain the relationship. In a long-distance relationship, what are the pros of using text messages to communicate with your partner? What are the cons?

Scene Two Length and Location: Approximately 2 minutes (0:14:25–0:16:05)
Opening Line: "My dad's a gynecologist in India."
Closing Line: "That was supposed to say that I like sports."

Discussion Questions

1. How frequently do misunderstandings occur via text messages? What have you learned that can help you avoid these misunderstandings?
2. Does texting have some benefits compared with face-to-face conversations? Make a list of these benefits and compare your list with someone else's.
3. What is in store for the future of technology and dating? Speculate what dating might be like 5 or 10 years from now. Will there be a greater reliance on technology? Possibly less?

BREAKING BAD

TV Show Data	
Year Began	2008
Number of Seasons	5
Creator(s)	Vince Gilligan
Genre	Crime Drama
Episode Length	47 Minutes

Main Cast	
Character	**Actor**
Walter White	Bryan Cranston
Skylar White	Anna Gunn
Jesse Pinkman	Aaron Paul
Hank Schrader	Dean Norris
Marie Schrader	Betsy Brandt
Walter White, Jr.	RJ Mitte

TV Show Storyline

Breaking Bad is known for having powerful writing and a fervent following. The show begins with Walter White, a brilliant high school chemistry teacher barely able to support his newly pregnant wife and teenage son. Shortly after turning 50, he is diagnosed with inoperable lung cancer. With nothing left to lose, he decides to start using his chemistry knowledge to cook meth and provide financially for his family. While on a ride-along with his DEA brother-in-law, Walt sees a former student, Jesse Pinkman, run from a crime scene and recognizes him. Walt then blackmails him into going into business with him.

Note: This series contains strong language.

Note: The location of each scene is based on viewing the episode without commercials (e.g., Amazon Instant Video, Hulu Plus, iTunes, Netflix, etc.). Each episode is approximately 47 minutes in length.

Season 1, Episode 1: "Pilot"

In this first scene for analysis, Walt and Jesse are just starting their meth-cooking partnership. Walt steals some equipment from the high school, and Jesse seems unimpressed with Walt's technical approach. This scene highlights the very different characters, and their different approaches to the same concepts—while cooking meth.

Central Concepts: Self-Concept, Language
Related Concepts: Perception, Identity Management

Length and Location of Scene One: Approximately 2 minutes (0:32:10–0:34:14)
Opening Line: "You just going to sit there?"
Closing Line: ". . . not me!"

Discussion Questions
1. How does Jesse react to being told what to do by Walt?
2. Does their conversation change their teacher/student dynamic?
3. How are they using language to convey their identities?

Season 3, Episode 10: "Fly"

In this scene, Walt and Jesse are in the middle of a "cook" when Walt finds a fly in the lab. Walt is trying to convince Jesse the fly is a problem. This scene highlights Walt's and Jesse's use of language, as well as how nonverbals communicate relational messages.

Central Concepts: Power, Relational Messages
Related Concepts: Language, Nonverbal Messages

Length and Location of Scene Two: Approximately 5 minute and 15 seconds (0:11:10–0:16:25)
Opening Line: "There's been a contamination."
Closing Line: "Okay."

Discussion Questions
1. There seems to be some confusion between Walt and Jesse about the problem. How do they express their confusion? What do you think was the cause of the confusion?
2. As Jesse notes, theirs is a "fifty-fifty partnership." Does it seem that way in how they interact? What is the power dynamic?

Season 5, Episode 6: "Buyout"

Jesse and Mike (a later addition to the business) want out of the business, and have an opportunity to sell their share of the stolen chemicals. Jesse, who does not visit Walt in his "other" life, is invited over to Walt's house to discuss the opportunity.

This scene is a continuation of the discussion of the buyout offer. In the middle of the conversation, Skylar, Walt's wife, arrives home. She has just visited with her sister and has discovered that Walt told her sister about an affair she had within the past year.

This scene can be divided into two. The first half looks at the relationship between Jesse and Walt, Jesse's attempts at persuasion, and Walt's emotional reaction. The second half of the scene watches the communication dynamic change dramatically with the entrance of Skylar.

Central Concepts: Communication Climate, Conflict, Relational Dynamics
Related Concepts: Self-disclosure, Nonverbal Communication

Length and Location of Scene One: Exactly 9 minutes (0:28:10–0:37:10)
Opening Line: (Walt opens the door.) "Yo, you sure this is OK?"
Closing Line: " . . . and you want to take it away from me."

Discussion Questions
1. How did Walt use self-disclosure in his conversation with Jesse?
2. How did Walt's and Jesse's communication patterns change from when they were alone to having Skylar present?
3. What relational messages were being sent at the dinner table?

HOUSE OF CARDS

TV Show Data	
Year Began	2013
Number of Seasons	3
Creator(s)	Beau Willimon
Genre	Political Drama
Episode Length	55 Minutes

Main Cast	
Character	**Actor**
Francis Underwood	Kevin Spacey
Clair Underwood	Robin Wright
Doug Stamper	Michael Kelly
Zoe Barnes	Kate Mara

TV Show Storyline

House of Cards is known for having a dedicated following. The show begins with Congressman Frank Underwood celebrating in the aftermath of a presidential election, having helped the candidate win the election. Though promised a nomination as Secretary of State, the new administration asks Frank to stay in Congress to help them move forward their legislative agenda. Although Frank agrees to support the President, he is angry about the snub and begins his own plans to move into increasingly more powerful positions.

Note: This series contains strong language.

Note: The location of each scene is based on viewing the episode without commercials (e.g., Amazon Instant Video, Hulu Plus, iTunes, Netflix, etc.). Each episode is approximately 47 minutes in length.

Season 1, Episode 1: "Chapter 1"

In this first scene for analysis, we see Frank and Clair interact after Frank had been avoiding Clair's calls. This is directly after Frank met with the new President's chief of staff, and was told he won't be getting nominated for Secretary of State.

Central Concept: Conflict
Related Concepts: Relational Messages, Emotional Expression
Length and Location of Scene One: Approximately 2 minutes (0:13:45–0:15:35)
Opening Line: "Clair. . . ."
Closing Line: "My husband doesn't apologize, even to me."

Discussion Questions
1. How are Frank and Clair expressing their emotions about the situation?
2. What disconfirming messages do we see them use?
3. What is the source of this conflict? What conflict style do they use?

Season 1, Episode 4: "Chapter 4"

In this scene, Clair and Frank discuss the possibility of a major donation to Clair's company. Clair is excited about the prospect of hiring back staff she had to fire after her company lost a donation when Frank wasn't nominated for Secretary of State, and the possibility of expanding the mission of her company. Frank is suspicious about the source of the donation.

Central Concepts: Conflict
Related Concepts: Power

Length and Location of Scene Two: Approximately 1 minute and 30 seconds (0:08:25–0:09:55)
Opening Line: "Hey . . . ."
Closing Line: "I'll tell you what I told him—I'll think about it."

Discussion Questions
1. How does this interaction reflect the definition of interpersonal conflict?
2. Who holds the power in this relationship? How do they attempt to exert power over one another?

MAD MEN

TV Show Data	
Year Began	2007
Number of Seasons	7
Creator(s)	Matthew Weiner
Genre	Period Drama
Episode Length	47 Minutes

Main Cast	
Character	**Actor**
Donald "Don" Draper	Jon Hamm
Peter "Pete" Campbell	Vincent Kartheiser
Joan P. Harris	Christina Hendricks
Roger H. Sterling, Jr.	John Slattery
Elizabeth "Betty" Draper	January Jones
Megan Draper	Jessica Paré
Margaret "Peggy" Olson	Elisabeth Moss
Sally Beth Draper	Kiernan Shipka

TV Show Storyline

Mad Men has garnered not only awards and critical acclaim but the public's fascination, for its historical authenticity, acting, writing, directing, costume and set design, and visual style. The show concentrates on the lives of a multitude of individuals living in the turbulent 1960s, from female secretaries, to ad men, to children. Don Draper is the show's main character, and the audience quickly becomes well-acquainted with him and his wife (Betty) and daughter (Sally). However, there are many other ancillary characters that, as the seasons progress, become main characters themselves. For example, the social climb of secretary-turned-creative force Peggy Olson; or stereotypical 1960s account man Pete Campbell, whose depth and complexity increase as his life unravels; or Don's daughter's coming of age amid her parents crumbling marriage. *Mad Men* becomes a landscape, littered with people and their daily struggles, both big and small.

Note: The location of each scene is based on viewing the episode without commercials (e.g., Amazon Instant Video, Hulu Plus, iTunes, Netflix, etc.). Each episode is approximately 47 minutes in length.

Season 3, Episode 11: "The Gypsy and the Hobo"

In this first scene for analysis, Betty has uncovered the truth about Don's identity (that he was originally Richard Whitman). In the midst of one of his affairs, Don comes home to quickly change, only to be confronted by Betty regarding documents she found in his desk. Don is choked with emotion, but proceeds to tell her about his mysterious past, involving the real Donald Draper and the Korean War. Her reaction, coupled with Don's response, provides perfect fodder for concepts such as self-disclosure and identity management. This is followed by a tenuous reconciliation between the two, as the episode ends with the entire family together, trick-or-treating.

Central Concepts: Self-Disclosure, Self-Concept/Identity Management
Related Concepts: Conflict, Family Communication, Honesty/Lying/Deception/Ethics, Nonverbal Communication, Relational Intimacy

Length and Location of Scene One: Approximately 3½ minutes (0:27:33–0:31:02)
Opening Line: "The pictures covered with other people's names?"
Closing Line: "Donald Draper."

Discussion Questions
1. Why is Don so averse to disclosing his true identity to Betty, his wife? What does this say about his relationship with her?
2. When Betty asks Don who he is, why does Don say "Donald Draper" initially?
3. Identify the different types of nonverbal communication shown in this scene.

Length and Location of Scene Two: Approximately 1 minute and 15 seconds (0:45:26–0:46:38)
Opening Line: "Do I look like a gypsy?"
Closing Line: "And who are you supposed to be?"

Discussion Questions
1. What does Don and Betty's interaction before they go outside say about marriage/relationships in the 1960s? What is the subtext of Don's saying "good"?
2. Describe the family dynamics in this scene. How do Don and Betty express themselves to each other? To the children? How do these interactions compare to those of your family?
3. Analyze the final line of the scene. What is the subtext of Carlton's question? Would you be able to answer this question?

Season 5, Episode 11: "The Other Woman"

The following two scenes are extremely interconnected in the context of the episode's narrative, which makes them exceptionally complementary. In the first scene for analysis, Pete approaches Joan with a salacious proposition. He suggests that she sleep with Herb Rennet, in order to win the Jaguar account. Joan is disgusted, yet Pete has planted the idea in her head. The second scene for analysis depicts Don pitching an idea to Herb and his partners. The entirety of his presentation is spliced with scenes of Joan following through with Pete's earlier request.

Note: The start time for the second scene was chosen so as to avoid the scene with suggested sexual content involving Joan and Herb. There is no nudity in this scene, and it is up to the instructor whether or not to screen Don's full presentation.

Central Concepts: Organizational Communication, Persuasion
Related Concepts: Conflict, Culture, Ethos/Pathos/Logos, Public Speaking, Gender and Sex Roles

Length and Location of Scene One: Approximately 2½ minutes (0:05:33–0:08:06)
Opening Line: "You're here early."
Closing Line: "I understand."

Discussion Questions
1. How does Pete's position within the ad agency (an account man) affect his communicative behaviors, especially when propositioning Joan? Is there an interrelatedness of organizational experiences?
2. Discuss the interrelated power relationships within this scene. How much is this relationship informed by the culture of the 1960s, pertaining specifically to gender and sex roles?

Length and Location of Scene Two: Approximately 45 seconds (0:32:54–0:33:27)
Opening Line: "This thing."
Closing Line: No dialogue. Pete looks over at Herb.

Discussion Questions
1. How does Don go about persuading Herb and the other gentleman from Jaguar? Which rhetorical devices does he employ, and why are they effective?
2. Examine Don's public speaking. What is it about the way he presents that makes him so successful?
3. Choose a product, and attempt to persuade the class to buy it. Examine the angle(s) you used to persuade your classmates.

MODERN FAMILY

TV Show Data	
Year Began	2009
Number of Seasons	7
Creator(s)	Steve Levitan, Christopher Lloyd
Genre	Situation Comedy
Episode Length	30 minutes

Main Cast	
Character	**Actor**
Jay Pritchett	Ed O'Neill
Gloria Delgado-Pritchett	Sofia Vergara
Claire Dunphy	Julie Bowen
Phil Dunphy	Ty Burrell
Mitchell Pritchett	Jesse Tyler Ferguson
Cameron Tucker	Eric Stonestreet
Manny Delgado	Rico Rodriguez
Luke Dunphy	Nolan Gould
Haley Dunphy	Ariel Winter

TV Show Storyline

If you have turned on your television recently, or watched popular TV shows online, then you are likely familiar with the situation comedy *Modern Family*. As the title suggests, the show is a collection of characters comprising a variety of family types. There is the more traditional family unit, consisting of husband Phil Dunphy, his wife Claire, and their children Haley, Alex, and Luke. There's also Mitchell (Claire's biological brother) and Cameron, two gay men who have an adopted child from Vietnam. Lastly, there's the patriarch of the entire show: Jay (biological father of Claire and Mitchell). Jay is divorced and remarried to a much younger woman, Gloria, who has a young son named Manny.

Most episode plots involve issues relevant to raising children, such as sibling rivalries, parental decisions, family conflict, and so on. Other storylines range from the mundane (what to wear on the first day of school) to the unusual (where to go for the family trip). The show is also shot in pseudo-documentary style, which allows the storylines to play out accompanied by the characters' analyses and confessions made directly to the camera. Not only do these moments make for humorous commentary, they also serve as examples of metacommunication.

Note: The location of each scene is based on viewing the episode without commercials (e.g., Amazon Instant Video, Hulu Plus, iTunes, etc.). Each episode is approximately 22 minutes in length.

Season 2, Episode 5: "Unplugged"

In this episode, Claire is fed up with her family's addiction to technology (e.g., cell phones, video games, and computers). In order to cure them of their affliction, Claire and Phil attempt a bold idea: no technology for anyone for an entire week, and whoever can go the longest without technology wins a prize. Soon enough the family members, including Phil and Claire, struggle to wean themselves of life's little electronic conveniences. It's anyone's guess who can hold out the longest.

Central Concept: Technology
Related Concepts: Computer-Mediated Communication

Length and Location of Scene One: Approximately 2 minutes (0:01:20–0:03:10)
Opening Line: "Okay, there you go."
Closing Line: "That's awesome."

Discussion Questions
1. Is the Dunphys' use of technology typical of most families today? Provide examples.
2. Claire exclaims that families are "supposed to talk" without technology. Does technology isolate family members from each other, or does technology bring them closer together? Please explain with examples.

Length and Location of Scene Two: Approximately 2 minutes (0:04:30–0:06:10)
Opening Line: "Okay, we have called this family meeting because the personal electronics have gotten out of control."
Closing Line: "I have almost no faith in you."

Discussion Questions
1. How dependent are you on technology?
2. Would it be possible for you to completely unplug from technology for more than a few days? Please explain.

Note: There are more scenes in this episode that close the Dunphy storyline on technology. These scenes were not mentioned here, mostly because they are humorous but offer little additional content for analysis.

Season 2, Episode 17: "Two Monkeys and a Panda"

This episode presents a so-called typical day for the Dunphy family—typical, at least, for Claire. Because while Claire is driving all over town running errands and trying to solve family crises, Phil is getting a make-over at a local beauty spa. Exasperated and practically at her wit's end, Claire telephones Phil and asks him to make dinner that night. Their conversation does not end well, and Phil is left bewildered about what went wrong. Fortunately for him, Phil just happens to be surrounded by a group of women who are more than willing to teach him the differences between male and female communication.

Central Concept: Gender
Related Concepts: Supportive Communication, Listening, Communication Climate

Length and Location of Scene One: Approximately 1 minute (0:08:18–0:09:25)
Opening Line: "I'm thinking of getting bangs."
Closing Line: "Hello? What?"

Discussion Questions
1. How would you describe Phil's style of talk? What is the goal of communication for Phil? Is his style typical of men? Please explain.
2. Place yourself in Claire's position. Why is she so upset after talking with Phil? How would you label Phil's listening style?
3. Explain how Phil should have spoken to Claire, focusing on gender styles and communication expectations.

Length and Location of Scene Two: Approximately 1½ minutes (0:12:30–0:13:54)
Opening Line: "Okay, I'm confused."
Closing Line: "Okay, now I'm confused again."

Discussion Questions
1. Do you agree or disagree with the advice these women gave to Phil? Why?
2. Do you agree or disagree with their analysis of female expectations for communication? Why?

Length and Location of Scene Three: Approximately 2 minutes (0:15:30–0:17:40)
Opening Line: "Is she back yet!?"
Closing Line: "I'll just go make dinner."

Discussion Questions
1. Evaluate Phil's style of talk now. Was he able to provide supportive communication for Claire? Please explain.
2. How would you label Phil's listening style now?

Season 3, Episode 13: "Little Bo Bleep"

One storyline in this episode centers on Claire running for City Council. The episode begins with a recent article in the local newspaper reporting that "Claire Dunphy is angry and unlikable." In order to improve her image and prepare for the election, Phil and the children suggest having a mock debate. That way, Claire can practice her talking points about the issues and polish her delivery skills. Additionally, her family can also point out all of her negative nonverbal cues. As you watch this scene, try to identify the different types of nonverbal cues that Claire exhibits. Is her family's criticism justified? When making a first impression, does nonverbal communication make that much of a difference?

Central Concepts: Nonverbal Communication
Related Concepts: Public Speaking

Length and Location of Scene: Approximately 3 minutes (0:04:35–0:07:25)
Opening Line: "Welcome, candidates."
Closing Line: *"She's ready."*

Discussion Questions
1. Identify the different functions of nonverbal communication (e.g., repeating, substituting, complementing, accenting, regulating, and contradicting) that Claire displays.
2. Label the types of nonverbal cues (kinesics, haptics, proxemics, etc.) that Claire displays.
3. Do you agree that nonverbal communication affects the perceptions of a political candidate's image or credibility? Recall and discuss an actual example when a politician's nonverbal communication influenced his or her credibility—either positively or negatively.

A second storyline in this episode, and a helpful bridge between nonverbal and verbal communication, concerns the use of inappropriate language. It seems that Lily, the young daughter of Mitchell and Cameron, has picked up on a certain swear word. When Lily drops the F-bomb in front of her parents, Mitchell is aghast while Cameron can barely contain his laughter. However, they are both concerned that Lily will embarrass them in public at an upcoming wedding, where Lily will be the flower girl. How do we learn language? And why do we seem to learn the inappropriate words first? Is Mitchell overreacting, or is Cameron out of touch with the seriousness of this issue?

Central Concepts: Language
Related Concepts: Rules of Language, Swearing

Length and Location of Scene One: Approximately 1 minute (0:07:25–0:08:40)
Opening Line: "And it's this."
Closing Line: "I have two children."

Discussion Questions

1. Which rules of language (phonetic, syntactic, semantic, or pragmatic) are demonstrated in this scene?
2. Have you ever witnessed a young child swearing? What was your reaction?
3. Do you agree with Mitchell that Lily should be told this is a bad word, or do you side with Cameron's advice to ignore the issue? Why?

Length and Location of Scene Two: Approximately 1 minute (0:11:15–0:12:30)
Opening Line: "Do you have any idea what station this is on?"
Closing Line: "We leave town on Gay Pride weekend because we don't like the traffic."

Discussion Questions

1. What is Lily's reason for using this word? What does this suggest about her understanding of language and meanings?
2. What is your opinion about adults using swear words? Is swearing ever okay? What about at home or with friends? In the workplace? Have you ever had a teacher swear in class? Was it appropriate or inappropriate? Why?

Season 3, Episode 14: "Me? Jealous?"

This episode begins with Phil and Claire entertaining a top real-estate agent (Tad, played by Greg Kinnear). Ultimately, Phil wants to join Tad's firm, since this should give Phil more access to higher-end properties on the market. Dinner with Tad goes well until he starts to leave, and he plants a firm kiss on Claire's lips. Surprisingly, Phil does not notice Tad's kiss. What follows is a humorous example of nonverbal expectancies, and the possible reactions when those expectancies are violated by someone else.

Central Concept: Nonverbal Communication
Related Concepts: Expectancy Violations, Regulative and Constitutive Rules, Jealousy

Length and Location of Scene One: Approximately 2½ minutes (0:02:05–0:03:45)
Opening Line: "Tad, this wine is fantastic."
Closing Line: "It's a progressive culture. Most of them travel by zip-line."

Discussion Questions

1. Given the context of the situation and the relationship between the characters, why is Tad's nonverbal communication unexpected for Claire?
2. Why is Phil blind to Tad's behavior?

Length and Location of Scene Two: Approximately 2 minutes (0:08:05–0:09:45)
Opening Line: "Honey, I'm home."
Closing Line: "Do you realize how insulting that is?"

Discussion Questions

1. After watching this second scene, now speculate why Phil is still blind to Tad's behavior. Use expectancy violations to explain your answer.
2. Describe a situation in which your perception of nonverbal communication was very different from someone else's perception. Why were these different perceptions present?

Length and Location of Scene Three: Approximately 3 minutes (0:18:05–0:20:40)
Opening Line: "Have a seat."
Closing Line: "I'd like to go back."

Discussion Questions

1. Use regulative and constitutive rules to explain Phil's reasons for leaving Tad's house.
2. For Claire, Phil's jealousy is a sign that he cares about her. In that way, could partner jealousy be a good thing? Why or why not?

ORANGE IS THE NEW BLACK

TV Show Data	
Year Began	2013
Number of Seasons	3
Creator(s)	Jenji Kohan
Genre	Comedy, Crime, Drama
Episode Length	55 minutes

Main Cast	
Character	**Actor**
Piper Chapman	Taylor Schilling
Alex Vause	Laura Prepon
Sam Healy	Michael J. Harney
Miss Claudette Pelage	Michelle Hurst
Galina "Red" Reznikov	Kate Mulgrew
Larry Bloom	Jason Biggs
Suzanne "Crazy Eyes" Warren	Uzo Aduba
Tasha "Taystee" Jefferson	Danielle Brooks
Nicole "Nicky" Nichols	Natasha Lyonne

TV Show Storyline

Based on Piper Kerman's memoir *Orange Is the New Black: My Year in a Women's Prison*, the series follows Piper Chapman, an upper middle class yuppie from New York who is sentenced to fifteen months in federal prison for transporting drug money for her ex-girlfriend Alex Vause (Laura Prepon). A decade after she commits the crime and two years before the statute of limitations on it runs out, Piper is thrust into prison life and a forced reunion with Alex.

Season 1, Episode 1: "I Wasn't Ready"

The pilot episode revolves around the protagonist's first days in prison and introduces a colorful cast of characters, from correctional officer Sam Healy [Michael J. Harney], who sees Piper as a welcome addition to the ward, to warmhearted yet tempestuous prison cook Red [Kate Mulgrew]. Scenes showing Piper's all-but-smooth transition into prison life are interspersed with flashbacks from her former one, revealing stark contrasts and the story behind her decade-old offense.

Central Concept: Culture Shock
Related Concepts: Expectancy Violation, Proxemics

Length and Location of Scene: Approximately 2 minutes (0:00:01–0:002:00)
Opening Line: "I've always loved getting clean."
Closing Line: "*[Singing]* Ain't nobody crying . . . Ain't nobody worried."

Discussion Questions
1. Describe Piper's experience of culture shock, including her loss of personal space. How does she adapt to her new circumstances?
2. Identify how violations of expectations are demonstrated in this scene. Is the loss of privacy an entirely negative violation for Piper?
3. Have you ever experienced culture shock, or a feeling of disorientation in a new and unfamiliar environment? Describe the situation and how you felt. Looking back, what did you learn to help you navigate similar situations in the future?

Season 1, Episode 6: "The WAC Pack"

In this episode, a scuffle over the television results in the revival of the women's advisory council, to be comprised of one representative from each ethnicity. In anticipation of the election, the inmates campaign for spots and engage in a rap battle for dominance.

Central Concept: Perception (Stereotyping and Prejudice)
Related Concepts: Identity, Culture

Length and Location of Scene: Approximately 4 minutes and 30 seconds (0:17:05–0:21:35)
Opening Line: "So I'm thinking campaign posters instead of buttons."
Closing Line: "Quiet down!"

Discussion Questions
1. Discuss the role that perception and stereotyping play in this scene. In what ways do the characters engage in stereotyping?
2. What is the basis for the group stereotypes illustrated here? Are they persistent? Are they warranted?
3. How does being part of a cultural or ethnic group influence your identity?

SECTION III
FULL-LENGTH FEATURE FILMS

Each of the film entries in this section provides information in the following categories:

Film Data: Year, Director, Length, and Rating
Cast: Principal roles in the film
Communication Courses: Appropriate classes for using the film (listed alphabetically)
Communication Concepts: Communication concepts that can be illustrated through the film (listed alphabetically)
Pedagogical Perspective: Introduction and viewing notes for the film, indicating audience
Synopsis: Summary of the film's plot and themes
Discussion Questions: Questions (and answers) linking the film to communication concepts

The discussion questions are the heart of this section. The questions posed are not the only ones that can or should be asked, nor are the answers given for the films the only "right" way to respond to the questions. In fact, you may argue with some of the analyses and interpretations. That's fine—any good discussion about movies should engender disagreement. The questions and answers are provided simply to offer you direction and data for analyzing the movies.

This book is designed as an ancillary for communication textbooks that focus on primarily on interpersonal and group communication concepts. Whenever possible, terms from these texts are used in the film entries, particularly in the discussion questions and their responses. The responses suggest some, but certainly not all, of the ways the discussion questions can be answered with concepts from the textbooks. It is likely that other communication issues beyond the ones identified can be found in the films. Thus, the entries should be seen as comprehensive but not exhaustive. If and when they stimulate new ideas, please share those ideas through letters, e-mail, papers, and articles.

(500) DAYS OF SUMMER

Film Data	
Year	2009
Director	Marc Webb
Length	95 minutes
Rating	PG-13

Main Cast	
Character	**Actor**
Tom Hansen	Joseph Gordon-Levitt
Summer Finn	Zooey Deschanel

Communication Concepts
Attachment Styles
Commitment
Nonverbal Miscommunication
Relational Development and Dialectics

Viewing Information
In an ominous tone, a voice utters the opening line of the film: "This is not a love story." Indeed, it is not. Tom Hansen is a shy, hopeless romantic who writes greeting card lines for a living. Seemingly out of nowhere, Summer Finn walks into his life, and Tom is smitten at first sight. One problem, though: Summer does not believe in romance. Tom pursues Summer anyway, and although they do become involved romantically, Tom learns several painful lessons about unrequited love. Remember, this is not a love story.

Synopsis
Tom Hansen thought he had found "the one." Like her seasonal namesake, Summer Finn blew into Tom's life unexpectedly, and he was a changed man—though perhaps not for the better. *(500) Days of Summer* opens with Tom severely depressed, mourning his break-up with Summer. In non-linear fashion, the rest of the film portrays Tom's reflections on their relationship leading up to, and after, their break-up. Along the way, we are treated to moments of misunderstood signals, ruminations on romance, and a conflict of commitment.

Discussion Questions

1. Identify Tom and Summer's stages of relational development, including their coming together and coming apart stages. How are differences in commitment demonstrated in these stages? How do the characters experience and manage the predictability versus novelty dialectic?

2. Use attachment styles theory to label Tom and Summer's perspectives on love and relationships, and identify examples of their attachment styles. Are their different attachment styles necessarily incompatible? Explain.

3. Locate moments when Tom has difficulty reading Summer's nonverbal cues. Does Tom have poor nonverbal decoding skills, or is Summer difficult to read? What are their content and relational level meanings?

AMERICAN HUSTLE

Film Data
Year: 2013
Director: David O. Russell
Length: 138 Minutes
Rated: R

Characters/Actors
Irving Rosenfeld: Christian Bale
Richard "Richie" DiMaso: Bradley Cooper
Sydney Prosser: Amy Adams
Mayor Carmine Polito: Jeremy Renner
Rosalyn Rosenfeld: Jennifer Lawrence

Communication Courses
Interpersonal Communication
Mass Media and Society

Communication Concepts
Public/Private Self and Identity Management
Self-Concept/Looking-Glass Self/Self-Fulfilling Prophecy
Stereotypes/Prototypes/Scripts
Confirming/Disagreeing/Disconfirming Messages
Communication Climate

Viewing Information
American Hustle is, in many ways, a period piece. From the hairstyles, to the wardrobes, to the soundtrack, director David O. Russell throws audiences back into the 1970s. Perhaps one of the most tantalizing aspects of the film is that there are five fully fledged, complex characters, each with neuroses, flaws, and endearing qualities. One could even argue that there are five main characters. *American Hustle* was released to critical acclaim, and for good reason. The film is rated R for sexual material, some violence, profanity, and scenes containing substance abuse—all depicted artfully, so as to capture the essence of a time period.

Synopsis
Loosely based on the FBI ABSCAM operation that took place as the 1970s transitioned into the 1980s, *American Hustle* centers on con artists Irving Rosenfeld and Sydney Prosser who are forced by FBI agent Richie DiMaso to engineer an intricate sting operation in an attempt to expose corrupt politicians. Richie's prime target becomes Camden, New Jersey's Mayor Carmine Polito. As Irving is pulled more and more deeply into a scam he knows is doomed to fail, he must not only negotiate the two women in his life—his current mistress and partner Sydney, and his unpredictable wife Rosalyn—but save himself and those around him from almost assured prosecution.

Discussion Questions

1. The five main characters (Irving, Richie, Sydney, Mayor Carmine, and Rosalyn) are wildly different individuals, each with strong personalities. What stereotype does each character fulfill? What scripts do the characters follow? Choose two of the five main characters and analyze their self-concept. Use the terms *looking-glass self* and *self-fulfilling prophecy* in your analysis.

2. Discuss self-concept in relation to *American Hustle*'s two leading female characters, Sydney Prosser (Amy Adams) and Rosalyn Rosenfeld (Jennifer Lawrence). Explain how their self-conceptions are similar and/or different.

3. *American Hustle* contains many volatile relationships. How is the idea of confirming/disagreeing/disconfirming messages, in the context of a relationship, present in the film? Which relationships best display this concept?

ARGO

Film Data	
Year	2012
Director	Ben Affleck
Length	120 minutes
Rating	R

Main Cast	
Character	**Actor**
Tony Mendez	Ben Affleck
Jack O'Donnell	Bryan Cranston
Lester Siegel	Alan Arkin
John Chambers	John Goodman
Bob Anders	Tate Donovan
Joe Stafford	Scoot McNairy
Kathy Stafford	Kerry Bishé
Lee Schatz	Rory Cochrane
Cora Lijek	Clea DuVall
Mark Lijek	Christopher Denham

Communication Concepts
Group Cohesiveness
Group Decision-Making
Group Roles
Leadership
Problem-Solving in Groups

Viewing Information
   Although based on actual events that occurred early in the Iran hostage crisis (1979-1981), *Argo* is a dramatization and fictionalized account of one particular group's experience. A suspense-thriller, the film stars and is directed by Ben Affleck. His character, Tony Mendez, hatches a plan to rescue six American diplomats who managed to avoid being taken hostage but are also trapped in Iran. In order to carry out his plan to bring them home, Mendez seeks help

from two major Hollywood players: special effects wizard John Chambers (John Goodman) and film producer Lester Siegel (Alan Arkin). Together, they intend to rescue the six diplomats with an implausible idea: pretend they are a Canadian film crew on location in Iran and fly them out on a commercial airliner. The film won the Oscar for Best Picture in 2013.

Synopsis

The year is 1979, and the American embassy in Iran has just been overrun by a large group of radical militants. These militants take 52 Americans hostage, but the U.S. State Department learns that six American diplomats managed to escape and that they are currently under the protection of the Canadian Ambassador to Iran. Tony Mendez is a CIA operative known for his expertise in "exfiltration"—getting American citizens out of a foreign occupied country. When the U.S. State Department consults Mendez on how to exfiltrate the six American diplomats, he offers an unusual solution: disguise the six diplomats as a Canadian film crew on location and fly them out on a commercial airliner. As implausible as the idea seems, Mendez receives the go-ahead from the U.S. government. Now he just has to convince the six diplomats to go along with his plan and carry out the mission before the Iranian government discovers their true identities.

Discussion Questions

1. Identify different stages of problem-solving that occur during the cabinet meetings with the U.S. Government officials. What specific steps do these groups take to solve problems? How does power influence this process?
2. Analyze the group communication among the six American diplomats, and examine their decision to follow Tony Mendez's plan. How does this group make decisions? Which group roles are demonstrated? How does group cohesiveness influence their decisions?
3. Consider Tony Mendez as a group leader. What traits does he possess that are typical of leaders? How would you describe his leadership style? How does Mendez adapt his style to match his followers (the six diplomats)?

THE BREAKFAST CLUB

Film Data	
Year	1985
Director	John Hughes
Length	92 minutes
Rating	R

Main Cast	
Character	**Actor**
Andrew Clark	Emilio Estevez
Richard Vernon	Paul Gleason
Brian Johnson	Anthony Michael Hall
John Bender	Judd Nelson
Claire Standish	Claire Standish
Allison Reynolds	Ally Sheedy

Communication Concepts
Critical Thinking
Group Cohesiveness
Group Development
Perception
Power
Roles
Self-Disclosure
Status

Viewing Information
The movie clearly subscribes to an "ideology of intimacy." The moral of the story appears to be that openness and honesty—even with complete strangers—will make a person happy, healthy, and wise. Something to think about as you watch the film is "Do you think the members of the Breakfast Club will remain friends?" While those who love happy endings may answer yes, many realistically acknowledge that peer pressure from the members' cliques will keep them from interacting on Monday. If this is true, then the five teenagers in the movie have handed intimate, personal, and private information to people who may be their social enemies (or at least competitors) at school. In a worst-case scenario, their self-disclosures could become inter-clique arsenal in the weeks that follow. The pros and cons of self-disclosure are an integral issue in *The Breakfast Club.*

Synopsis

The Breakfast Club takes place at an Illinois high school, where five dissimilar students are sentenced to spend a Saturday detention session together. In attendance is a "princess" (Ringwald), an "athlete" (Estevez), a "brain" (Hall), a "criminal" (Nelson), and a "basket case" (Sheedy). These titles identify the roles the students play during the school week. Because of stereotypes and status levels associated with each role, the students want nothing to do with each other at the outset of the session. However, when confronted by the authoritarian detention teacher (Gleason) and by eight hours of time to kill, the students begin to interact. Through self-disclosure they learn that they are more similar than different. Each wrestles with self-acceptance; each longs for parental approval; each fights against peer pressure. They break through the role barriers and gain greater understanding and acceptance of each other and of themselves. They ultimately develop a group identity and dub themselves "The Breakfast Club."

Discussion Questions

1. How do the characters deviate from their normal roles during the detention session?
2. What is the status of each character prior to the detention session? How does this change during their detention session?
3. What power resources and discussion roles are exhibited in the movie?
4. Discuss the group's developmental stages.
5. What factors contribute to the group's cohesiveness?
6. Discuss the role that perception and stereotyping play in this movie.

THE BREAK-UP

Film Data	
Year	2006
Director	Peyton Reed
Length	106 minutes
Rating	PG-13

Main Cast	
Character	**Actor**
Gary Grobowski	Vince Vaughn
Brooke Meyers	Jennifer Aniston
Addie	Joey Lauren Adams
Johnny O	Jon Favreau
Marilyn Dean	Judy Davis
Dennis Grobowski	Vincent D'Onofrio
Lupus Grobowski	Cole Hauser

Communication Concepts

Conflict Management Styles
Content- and Relational-Level Meanings
Language Styles (low- and high-context)
Listening Responses (supportive and non-supportive)
Relational Dialectics (independence-autonomy)
Relational Stages

Viewing Information

Why do women and men struggle to understand each other? And why can it be so difficult to tell our partners how we really feel? This unconventional romantic comedy attempts to answer these, and other, questions regarding the coming apart stages of interpersonal relationships.

Synopsis

The Break-Up is a unique romantic comedy. Instead of the usual happily-ever-after plot, the film portrays what can happen when a couple struggles with the end of their relationship. Brooke is an art gallery assistant who wants more than anything else to have Gary want to work on their relationship. Gary is a tour bus guide who wants more than anything else to be left alone. The two are so incompetent in their attempts to repair their relationship it's no wonder they end in a break-up.

Discussion Questions

1. Identify the relational stages and dialectical tensions Gary and Brooke experience, and describe how these lead to their break-up.
2. Describe the supportive and non-supportive messages directed at Gary and Brooke by their friends and family members.
3. Explain how both low- and high-context language styles are present in the film.
4. Identify the styles of conflict used by Brooke and Gary.

BRIDGET JONES'S DIARY

Film Data	
Year	2001
Director	Sharon McGuire
Length	98 minutes
Rating	R

Main Cast	
Character	**Actor**
Bridget Jones	Renee Zellweger
Mark Darcy	Colin Firth
Daniel Cleaver	Hugh Grant
Bridget's Mum	Gemma Jones
Bridget's Dad	Jim Broadbent

Communication Concepts
Communication Competence
Self-Concept

Viewing Information
This is a fun film that resonates with young women. Bridget's obsession with her weight, appearance, and clothing will ring true for many college-age females who are bombarded with interpersonal and media messages about thinness, beauty, and apparel. The movie also raises interesting questions about what Bridget wants in a relationship: Does she want a "good man" (Mark) or a "bad boy" (Daniel)? It appears she wants both—and the final lines of the movie suggest that Mark might be able to fill both roles. The movie is rated R for language (liberal use of the "f-word") and sexuality (including a brief nude scene).

Synopsis
Bridget Jones (Zellweger) is a single British woman in her early 30s who worries that she will die "fat and alone." By her own admission she drinks too much, smokes too much, and is overweight—all factors contributing to her fragile self-esteem. Her self-concept and communication competence (or lack thereof) are central features in her relationships with Mark Darcy (Firth) and Daniel Cleaver (Grant), both of whom vacillate between courting and dumping Bridget in a variety of romantic (and humorous) encounters. By the end of the film, Bridget decides which man truly loves her—and that she likes herself "just as she is."

Discussion Questions
1. Describe how Bridget's self-concept is constructed (and deconstructed/reconstructed) through reflected appraisal and social comparison.
2. Describe Bridget's communication competence/incompetence in interpersonal, public speaking, and interviewing situations.

CATFISH

Film Data	
Year	2010
Director	Henry Joost, Ariel Schulman
Length	87 minutes
Rating	PG-13

Main Cast	
Character	**Actor**
Yaniv (Nev) Schulman	Himself
Ariel (Rel) Schulman	Himself
Henry Joost	Himself
Angela Wesselman-Pierce	Herself
Melody C. Roscher	Herself

Communication Concepts
Computer-Mediated Communication
Deception
Self-Disclosure

Social Information Processing

Viewing Information
When filmmaker Ariel Shulman noticed that his brother, Yaniv (Nev) Shulman, was falling for a young woman he met online, Ariel thought it would be a great story for a short film. Along with friend and fellow filmmaker Henry Joost, Ariel began to chronicle every moment of Nev's budding online romance. And when Nev travels to meet this woman in person, Ariel and Henry are there to capture the anticipated feel-good moment. What actually transpires at this meeting, however, is something no one could have predicted.

Synopsis
Like many of his contemporaries, New Yorker Yaniv (Nev) Shulman is not a neophyte when it comes to using technology. Armed with their laptops and smart phones, young people are constantly connected to each other. When he begins an online friendship with a young girl (Abbey Wesselman) in Michigan who likes his photography, Nev is flattered. And when he starts an online relationship with Abbey's older sister, Megan, Nev is smitten. Through months of wall

postings, email messages, and phone calls, Nev's attraction to Megan blossoms into a fully committed intimate relationship. The anticipation builds as Nev and Megan plan their first face-to-face meeting in Michigan. Watch how this documentary, filmed by Nev's brother (Ariel Shulman) and close friend (Henry Joost), witnesses the twists and turns of Nev's online romance.

Discussion Questions

1. Compare Nev and Megan's relationship through computer-mediated communication (CMC) with a typical relationship that develops face-to-face (FTF). In what ways are CMC and FTF relationships similar? How are they different?

2. How did the use of CMC and social networking sites (e.g., Facebook) influence the characters' construction of their identities? How are their public and private selves aligned, or out of sync? Is your own social networking site profile an accurate reflection of your offline self?

3. Compared with face-to-face interactions, how much deception occurs online? Speculate how Megan was able to deceive Nev so completely and for so long. What features of CMC interactions enabled Megan to achieve this deception, and why didn't Nev catch on sooner?

THE DEVIL WEARS PRADA

Film Data	
Year	2006
Director	David Frankel
Length	109 minutes
Rating	PG-13

Main Cast	
Character	**Actor**
Miranda Priestly	Meryl Streep
Andy Sachs	Anne Hathaway
Emily	Emily Blunt
Nigel	Stanley Tucci
Christian Thompson	Simon Baker

Communication Concepts
Defensive Communication
Listening Behaviors
Organizational Culture
Self-Presentation

Viewing Information
The Oscar-nominated film *The Devil Wears Prada* is a fun and enjoyable film. Almost anyone will easily relate to the character of Andy Sachs and be amused by Miranda Priestly's obviously poor interpersonal communication skills. Examples abound in this funny and dramatic 2006 film, making it simple to glean lessons for how to (and how to not) behave in the workplace.

Synopsis
Recent college graduate Andrea Sachs (Hathaway) becomes an assistant to the mercilessly demanding fashion magazine editor Miranda Priestly (Streep). In nearly every interaction between Priestly and Sachs, the self-absorbed boss demonstrates that she values herself more than others and cares little about communicating competently or positively. The workaholic diva harshly criticizes all of her underlings, ignores their contributions, speaks cruelly, dismisses them or leaves the room in mid-sentence. Priestly offers few positive cues (verbal and nonverbal) in exchanges with her colleagues.

Discussion Questions

1. Which of Gibb's defense-provoking behaviors are utilized by Miranda Priestly?
2. Describe Miranda Priestly's listening behaviors.
3. Describe some of the messages about body image and body distortion issues present in the film.
4. What disconfirming messages does Andrea send to her boyfriend and friends once her work at the magazine becomes her major focus?

EASY A

Film Data	
Year	2010
Director	Will Gluck
Length	25 minutes
Rating	PG-13

Main Cast	
Character	**Actor**
Olive Penderghast	Emma Stone
Marianne	Amanda Bynes
Rhiannon	Alyson Michalka
Mr. Griffith	Thomas Haden Church
Mrs. Griffith	Lisa Kudrow
Rosemary Penderghast	Patricia Clarkson
Dill Penderghast	Stanley Tucci

Communication Concepts
Computer-Mediated Communication
Face Maintenance
Identity Management

Viewing Information
Set and filmed on location in idyllic Ojai, California, *Easy A* stars Emma Stone is Olive Penderghast: a once invisible high school student, now with a bad reputation. Intentionally written to resemble a John Hughes movie from the 1980s (*Ferris Bueller's Day Off, Pretty in Pink, Sixteen Candles*), this comedy explores how high school rumors get started, how they spread, and their strong influence on perceptions. The film also has a star-studded ensemble cast, including Stanley Tucci and Patricia Clarkson as Olive's parents, Thomas Haden Church as her favorite teacher, and Lisa Kudrow as the school guidance counselor.

Synopsis
Easy A recounts the tale of Olive Penderghast, a clean-cut high school girl whose reputation quickly takes a turn for the worse. When Olive lies to her best friend about losing her virginity, the school's rumor mill takes over. Olive's image is transformed seemingly overnight, and she

starts to notice that her life resembles that of Hester Prynne, Nathaniel Hawthorne's adulteress in *The Scarlet Letter*. Recognizing that she can capitalize both financially and socially on her new status, Olive embraces the role. However, she soon realizes that pretending to be an overly sexualized teenager is a lot more fun than actually being one. Having lost her best friend and on the verge of being expelled, can Olive squash these rumors and repair her lost identity?

Discussion Questions

1. Identify examples of Olive's identity management. How does Olive's perceived self compare to her presenting self, and how do these two selves change during the course of the film?
2. How do the characters engage in facework? Which characters are more concerned about their public face? Which characters are willing to give face to others?
3. *Easy A* illustrates how quickly a rumor can travel. Thinking about rumors specifically and information in general, how has technology changed the way information flows among people? How does the channel (e.g., texting) affect both the credibility of the source and the information itself?

GRAN TORINO

Film Data	
Year	2008
Director	Clint Eastwood
Length	116 minutes
Rating	R

Main Cast	
Character	**Actor**
Walt Kowalski	Clint Eastwood
Thao	Bee Vang
Sue	Ahney Her
Father Janovich	Christopher Carley
Barber Martin	John Carroll Lynch
Mitch Kowalski	Brian Haley

Communication Concepts
Adapting to Diversity
Linguistic Divergence/Convergence
Speech Codes Theory

Viewing Information

Veteran actor Clint Eastwood directs himself in this story about one man's resistance to changes in his neighborhood, and changes in his life. Not unlike his many past performances as an outlaw cowboy or police officer operating on the fringe, Eastwood's character in *Gran Torino* is a reluctant hero. He has little time or patience for people who are not like him, and he is not shy about expressing his discontent. Through interpersonal communication Eastwood not only learns to tolerate his new neighbors, he gains intercultural understanding as well. In the end, *Gran Torino* provides a moral lesson in both sacrifice and acceptance.

Synopsis

Eastwood plays Walt Kowalski, a retired autoworker and Korean War veteran living out his remaining days at his home. In Walt's world, nothing is supposed to change: children should always respect their elders, a man should be able take care of his own home, and people should live with their own kind. Walt's worldview changes dramatically when he gets to know his Hmong neighbors, and becomes an unwilling mentor for Thao, a young Hmong man in need of direction. Despite his crusty exterior and callous demeanor, Walt becomes both hero and savior for the entire neighborhood.

Discussion Questions

1. Analyze Walt's process of adapting to cultural diversity, including resistance, tolerance, and understanding. Identify differences between Walt's culture and the Hmong people.
2. Looking closely at Walt's communication style, how would you describe his language? What are the meanings and purposes Walt attaches to talk? Finally, contrast Walt's communication style with Thao's and Sue's.
3. Using speech codes theory, analyze Walt's personal and social identity. Identify examples when Walt teaches these speech codes to Thao.

THE GREAT DEBATERS

Film Data	
Year	2007
Director	Denzel Washington
Length	126 minutes
Rating	PG-13

Main Cast	
Character	**Actor**
Melvin B. Tolson	Denzel Washington
Henry Lowe	Nate Parker
Samantha Booke	Jurnee Smollett
James Farmer, Jr	Denzel Whitaker
Dr. James Farmer, Sr	Forest Whitaker
Hamilton Burgess	Jermaine Williams
Sheriff Dozier	John Heard

Communication Concepts
Leadership
Persuasive Appeals (Ethos, Pathos, Logos)
Power in Groups
Small Group Cohesiveness
Social Judgment Theory

Viewing Information
Based on the true story of the 1935 Wiley College Debate Team, this film is a dramatic account of confronting intolerance through speech. With eloquent oratory, the film illustrates well how persuasion can be used to change minds, and history. Students should recognize Denzel Washington and Forest Whitaker in their respective roles as debate coach and professor. However, it is the cast of young actors portraying the debate team who deserves consideration.

Synopsis
The Great Debaters is a moving, inspirational story about how the power of speech can overcome prejudice. The film is set in southern Texas in the 1930s, a time and place of racial intolerance, where Jim Crow laws were still on the books and lynchings were a common spectacle. At small, historically-black Wiley College, students on the debate team not only challenge each

other, they confront the prevailing social ideologies head-on. With the help of their charismatic and eloquent coach, real-life poet Melvin B. Tolson, the Wiley College Debate Team gains national recognition as one of the first black colleges to debate white students. Their prominence culminates with a nationally broadcast debate with Harvard University. In the end the debaters gain more than a simple victory, they gain respect for themselves and their race.

Discussion Questions
1. Identify examples of social judgment theory, including latitudes of acceptance, rejection, and non-commitment. How does ego-involvement influence the persuasive process?
2. How do the debaters utilize appeals to ethos, pathos, and logos in their arguments? Which type of appeal do you find most persuasive? Why?
3. Explain the factors or reasons why the Wiley College Debaters become a cohesive group.
4. Identify examples of power used by the characters. Which types of power are effective? Which types are appropriate?

THE KIDS ARE ALL RIGHT

Film Data	
Year	2010
Director	Lisa Cholodenko
Length	105 minutes
Rating	R

Main Cast	
Character	**Actor**
Nic	Annette Bening
Jules	Julianne Moore
Joni	Mia Wasikowska
Laser	Josh Hutcherson
Paul	Mark Ruffalo

Communication Concepts
Communication Conflict
Content and Relational Messages
Metacommunication
Relational Control

Viewing Information

Have you ever felt that your family is the only one with parents who constantly nag you, or who never seem to understand where you're coming from? Well, think again. In the film *The Kids Are All Right*, Director Lisa Cholodenko presents the typical American family. Yes, the parents happen to be two gay women (played by Julianne Moore and Annette Bening) who each gave birth to a child (played by Josh Hutcherson and Mia Wasikowska, respectively) from the same sperm donor, but push those details aside. Otherwise, you might miss the film's relevant and nuanced examples of family communication. And you might just realize that your own annoying parents actually care an awful lot about you.

Synopsis

Nic and Jules are living the American family script: two successful, upper-middle class parents raising their two children in Southern California. Joni, the older child, is about to head off to college, and her brother Laser is quickly becoming a young man. By the way, Nic and Jules are two gay women who gave birth to their children with the same sperm donor. When Laser pressures Joni to make contact with Paul, the donor, their entire family system is thrown off balance. Through conflicts brought on by Paul's influence and misunderstood intentions, Nic and Jules struggle to redefine their changing relationship and let go of their independence-craving children.

Discussion Questions

1. Identify examples of metacommunication Nic and Jules use in their relationship. Are these metamessages effective in solving their conflicts? Please explain.
2. Locate examples of content and relational messages. When are there misunderstandings between what was said, and how it was said? What effect do these misunderstandings have on the relationships among the characters?
3. Take a close look at all four family members, and analyze their different combinations of relational control. Which relationships are complementary? Which are symmetrical? Provide examples.

KNOCKED UP

Film Data	
Year	2007
Director	Judd Apatow
Length	133 minutes
Rating	R

Main Cast	
Character	**Actor**
Ben Stone	Seth Rogen
Alison Scott	Katherine Heigl
Pete	Paul Rudd
Debbie	Leslie Mann

Communication Concepts
Gendered Language
Relational Dialectics Theory
Relationship Stages and Commitment
Uncertainty Reduction Theory

Viewing Information
  Knocked Up will never be confused with a storybook romantic comedy. On the contrary, the appeal of the film is its modern take on dating, commitment, and the responsibilities of adulthood. Rogen's performance as slacker Ben Stone is classic Judd Apatow material, and Heigl as Alison Scott is a breakout role from her *Grey's Anatomy* character on television. Embedded within all the one-liners about sex and drugs lies a film with a message: Be prepared to change your approach—including your communication—when life throws you a curveball.

Synopsis
  Ben Stone is the quintessential slacker: he doesn't have a real job and spends most of his time smoking pot with his like-minded friends. Alison Scott, on the other hand, is the anti-Ben. Smart, attractive, and successful in her work, Alison seems to have the world at her feet. Out on the town celebrating her promotion, Alison meets and has a one-night-stand with Ben. The next day she realizes her mistake and ends their relationship. There's just one minor detail—she later discovers she's pregnant with Ben's child. In an effort to do what's right for their baby, Alison and Ben become a couple. What follows is a comedy about commitment, responsibility, and the realization that life doesn't care about the plans that you make.

Discussion Questions

1. Use uncertainty reduction theory to analyze conversations between Alison and Ben as they get to know each other.
2. Apply Knapp's stages of development and decline to the relationship between Alison and Ben.
3. Which relational dialectics are Debbie and Pete experiencing? How are they choosing to manage their dialectics?
4. What gendered language differences are present in the conversations among Alison, Ben, Debbie, and Pete?

LARS AND THE REAL GIRL

Film Data	
Year	2007
Director	Craig Gillespie
Length	106 minutes
Rating	PG-13

Main Cast	
Character	**Actor**
Lars	Ryan Gosling
Karin	Emily Mortimer
Gus	Paul Schneider
Dr. Dagmar	Patricia Clarkson
Margo	Kelli Garner

Communication Concepts
Coordinated Management of Meaning Theory
Relational Dialectics
Relationship Stages
Symbolic Interactionism Theory

Viewing Information
If you only read the DVD jacket of *Lars and the Real Girl*, you might conclude that the plot is hard to believe. On the contrary, this critically acclaimed film provides touching moments of community support and interpersonal understanding. Gosling gives a memorable performance as Lars, a delusional man searching for intimacy.

Synopsis
Lars Lindstrom is a shy, sweet man who lives by himself in his brother's garage. When Lars brings his new girlfriend (Bianca) home to meet his brother (Gus) and sister-in-law (Karin), they are thrilled—until they learn that she is an anatomically correct mannequin. At the urging of their family doctor, Gus and Karin go along with Lars' delusion. Eventually, the whole town treats Lars and Bianca as if their relationship is real. The film shows how an entire community can come together to support one individual, and how communication works to create our reality.

Discussion Questions

1. Do Lars and Bianca have a "real" interpersonal relationship?
2. Apply Knapp's stages of development and decline to the relationship between Lars and Bianca.
3. Using symbolic interactionism theory (meaning, language, and thought), describe how the characters co-construct their reality through communication. How does the community of townspeople, the generalized other, contribute to the film's narrative?
4. Apply Coordinated Management of Meaning (CMM) theory to the film by explaining the regulative and constitutive rules the characters follow, including both coordinated and uncoordinated meanings.

LITTLE MISS SUNSHINE

Film Data	
Year	2006
Director	Valerie Faris, Jonathan Dayton
Length	101 minutes
Rating	R

Main Cast	
Character	**Actor**
Olive Hoover	Abigail Breslin
Richard Hoover	Greg Kinnear
Dwayne	Paul Dano
Grandpa Edwin Hoover	Alan Arkin
Sheryl Hoover	Toni Collette
Frank Ginsberg	Steve Carell

Communication Concepts
Confirming/Disconfirming Communication
Family Communication
Self-Concept Formation
Self-Disclosure

Viewing Information
This heart-warming, popular film first strikes most viewers with the sheer dysfunction of its family members; but the hilarity of the situations coupled with the personal growth of its characters increases its applicability to interpersonal communication concepts. There is some sexual and drug content.

Synopsis
Little Miss Sunshine chronicles the adventures of 7-year-old Olive (Breslin) and her dysfunctional family as they travel from New Mexico to California, where Olive is to compete in the Little Miss Sunshine beauty contest. Olive's relatives are so burdened with their own quirks and neuroses that making it to California sane, alive, and on time for the pageant is uncertain until the end of the film. From tensions revealed early in the movie (i.e., the explosive dinner scene), it's clear that the 800-mile journey could do irreparable harm to each family member, and to all of their strained relationships. Along the way, the Hoover family members experience profound

changes, individually and collectively, as they all begin to share closely held personal secrets and experiences—and in so doing grow closer.

Discussion Questions

1. Describe the disconfirming messages presented by the various characters in the film.
2. Describe the confirming messages presented by Sheryl in the film.
3. Describe how the characters disclose personal information throughout the trip and how that disclosure enhances their relationships.
4. How did the family members bond and find a sense of cohesiveness in the 800-mile journey?
5. Describe Olive's self-concept and body image.

MONEYBALL

Film Data	
Year	2011
Director	Bennett Miller
Length	133 minutes
Rating	PG-13

Main Cast	
Character	**Actor**
Billy Beane	Brad Pitt
Peter Brand	Jonah Hill
Art Howe	Philip Seymour Hoffman
Grady Fuson	Ken Medlock
David Justice	Stephen Bishop

Communication Concepts
Leadership
Power in Groups
Problem Solving in Groups

Viewing Information

Brad Pitt is Billy Beane, the cunning yet charming General Manager of the Oakland Athletics Major League Baseball team. Based on Michael Lewis's book by the same name, *Moneyball* is set during the team's 2002 baseball season. The film chronicles their remarkable success on the field, and the secret formula that built the team. Sprinkled with clips of actual baseball games and cast with actors playing real baseball players, *Moneyball* is especially appealing for the sports enthusiast. Rounding out the cast, Peter Brand (Jonah Hill) is Beane's statistical genius, and Art Howe (Philip Seymour Hoffman) is the Athletics player Manager.

Synopsis

It is the 2001 Major League Baseball playoffs, and the cash-strapped Oakland Athletics have just lost to the money-rich New York Yankees. General Manager of the Athletics, Billy Beane (Brad Pitt), is beside himself with frustration and borderline anger. When it's time to assemble the 2002 team, and he learns that his star players are leaving for higher-paying contracts, Beane feels lost. On a scouting trip Beane meets Peter Brand (Jonah Hill), a recent Yale graduate with an economics degree and an apparent savant for baseball statistics. Brand eventually convinces

Beane to adopt his formula for evaluating players. What follows is a remarkable season by a most improbable team of misfits and castoffs who comprise the 2002 Oakland Athletics.

Discussion Questions

1. Identify examples of group problem solving, particularly during Beane's meetings with his scouts. What specific steps does the group take to make decisions? Which group roles are demonstrated?
2. Consider Billy Beane as a leader. What traits does he possess that are typical of leaders? How would you describe his leadership style? In what ways does his style change throughout the film?
3. How does Billy Beane demonstrate power in the film? What about his scouts and coaches? How does this create conflict?

OFFICE SPACE

Film Data	
Year	1999
Director	Mike Judge
Length	88 minutes
Rating	R

Main Cast	
Character	**Actor**
Peter Gibbons	Ron Livingston
Joanna	Jennifer Aniston
Milton Waddams	Stephen Root
Samir Nagheenanajar	Ajay Naidu
Michael Bolton	David Herman
Bill Lumbergh	Gary Cole

Communication Concepts
Classical Theory/Theory X
Communication Climate
Conflict
Honesty/Lying
Language
Self-Concept/Identity Management

Viewing Information

The back cover of the *Office Space* video proudly announces that the film is by Mike Judge, creator of *Beavis and Butt-head*, which should serve as a warning that the movie has some crude content and language (as well as two brief sexual scenes). While this is a very humorous film, it touches on some serious issues that can be explored. (For example, see "Investigating the Relationship Between Superior–Subordinate Relationship Quality and Employee Dissent" by J. W. Kassing in *Communication Research Reports* [2000], Vol. 17, pp. 58–69).

One of the unstated morals of *Office Space* is that Peter's life becomes better when he stops closely managing his identity and begins doing and saying whatever he wants. While this makes for an entertaining movie (and is the premise for other entertaining films such as *Liar Liar*), the outcomes of Peter's decisions can and should be a point of discussion for communication students. Would Peter actually be promoted to management if he ignored his boss, came to work whenever he wanted, dressed in shorts, destroyed company property, and admitted his lack of motivation to outside consultants? Probably only in Hollywood, which makes this a good case study for debating the pros and cons of identity management, honesty, and rhetorical sensitivity in the workplace.

Synopsis

Peter Gibbons (Livingston) and his colleagues Samir (Naidu) and Michael (Herman) are computer specialists who are fed up with their mundane jobs. They work at Initech Corporation, an impersonal organization with a Classical Theory/Theory X approach to management. Their boss, Lumbergh (Cole), has a condescending attitude and creates a defensive communication climate with all employees, including Milton (Root), the emotionally challenged mailroom clerk who keeps threatening to "burn the building." In a hypnotherapy session, Peter loses his inhibitions and starts speaking his mind around the office. His "straight shooting" earns him a promotion while others are downsized out of the company. Peter and his colleagues carry out a high-tech embezzling scheme to get revenge on Initech. Peter's new girlfriend, Joanna (Aniston), is also fed up with her waitress job and her manager; however, she helps Peter realize that embezzling is an unethical way to handle his frustration with Initech. Ultimately, Peter and his friends move on to new horizons and Initech (quite literally) goes up in flames.

Discussion Questions

1. Describe how the Initech Corporation illustrates Classical Theory and Theory X approaches to organizational communication.
2. Describe the communication climate in manager–employee interactions in the movie.
3. What styles of conflict management are used by the managers and employees in the movie?
4. Describe the changes Peter experiences in his identity management.

OUTSOURCED

Film Data	
Year	2006
Director	John Jeffcoat
Length	103 minutes
Rating	PG-13

Main Cast	
Character	**Actor**
Todd Anderson	Josh Hamilton
Asha	Ayesha Dharker
Puro	Asif Basra
Dave	Matt Smith

Communication Concepts
Adapting to Diversity
Culture Shock
Individualism and Collectivism
Organizational Culture
Proxemics

Viewing Information
A light-hearted comedy with a likable cast, *Outsourced* provides examples of contemporary business practices in the same way *Office Space* put the spotlight on the cubicle culture. Part cross-cultural sojourn and part international business, the film attempts to capture what happens when your job, and everyone who works for you, is outsourced to India. Hamilton portrays the business everyman, Dharker is his opinionated love interest, and Basra is Todd's charming and energetic replacement.

Synopsis
So far, the life of Todd Anderson has been predictable and uneventful. He manages a customer service call center in Seattle, for a company selling novelty products. However, his world is turned upside down when his job, and everyone under him, is outsourced to India. If being fired weren't bad enough, Todd's boss strong-arms him into going to India to train his replacement. In India Todd is overwhelmed by the cultural differences, both in and out of the new call center. He eventually finds a way to train his new staff and increase their productivity, but not before Todd learns something about himself.

Discussion Questions

1. Identify examples of Todd's culture shock, including his loss of personal space. Also, apply Edward Hall's distances in your explanation.
2. Recognize examples of Todd's individualism and the host culture's collectivism.
3. Provide examples that illustrate Todd's process of adapting to cultural diversity (i.e., resistance, tolerance, understanding, respect, and participation).
4. Analyze the organizational culture of the call center when Todd first arrives compared to the end of the film, including their rituals and customs. How was Todd able to motivate the employees and change their organizational culture?

SILVER LININGS PLAYBOOK

Film Data	
Year	2012
Director	David O. Russell
Length	124 minutes
Rating	R

Main Cast	
Character	**Actor**
Pat Solitano, Jr.	Bradley Cooper
Tiffany	Jennifer Lawrence
Pat Solitano, Sr.	Robert De Niro
Dolores Solitano	Jacki Weaver
Jake Solitano	Shea Whigham
Ronnie	John Ortiz

Communication Concepts
Communication Climate
Communication Competence
Conflict
Family Communication

Viewing Information
Silver Linings Playbook is a romantic comedy unlike most other films of the genre. Indeed, when one of the protagonists (Pat Jr., played by Bradley Cooper) suffers from bipolar disorder, and the other (Tiffany, played by Jennifer Lawrence) takes medication for severe depression, their interpersonal communication is sure to be unique. And let's not forget that Pat's father (Robert De Niro) is a highly superstitious gambler whose behavior borders on obsessive-compulsive disorder. When his mother (Dolores, played by Jacki Weaver) brings Pat home following a stay in a mental health facility, the family's interaction patterns are combustible. Surprisingly, Tiffany might be the antidote this family needs to help cure their dysfunctional communication.

Synopsis

Pat always knew in the back of his mind that he had undiagnosed mental health problems. Unfortunately for him, he had to lose his job, his marriage, and his freedom before he sought treatment for his bipolar disorder. When he is released from a mental health facility into his mother's custody, Pat swears that he wants to get his life back on track. Despite his estranged wife's restraining order against him, Pat intends to prove to her that he is a different, better person, beginning with a letter he intends to send her. In order to do this, however, Pat has to make a bargain with Tiffany, a mysterious friend of his wife's who has some mental issues of her own. Tiffany is a dancer, and she needs Pat to be her partner for an upcoming dance competition. Although very reluctant, Pat agrees to the compromise, and Tiffany promises to get Pat's letter to his wife. But as they practice together, something unexpected happens to Pat: dancing with Tiffany helps him stay focused and grounded. Ironically, Tiffany—a mysterious, depressed, and at times very outspoken woman—might just be the silver lining Pat is searching for.

Discussion Questions

1. How would you describe Pat's communication competence? What about Tiffany's? In several scenes, the characters argue that the other one is "crazier" or "says more inappropriate things" than the other. Who is right?
2. Choose one of the characters in the film (Pat, Tiffany, Pat Sr., Dolores, or Ronnie) and analyze their approach to conflict. Which conflict style does this character use most often? How effective is their conflict style?
3. Describe the Solitano family's communication patterns (this includes Pat, Pat Sr., Dolores, and Jake). How is this family a system? Are they interdependent? What are their interaction patterns?

SPANGLISH

Film Data	
Year	2004
Director	James L. Brooks
Length	131 minutes
Rating	PG-13

Main Cast	
Character	**Actor**
John Clasky	Adam Sandler
Deborah Clasky	Téa Leoni
Flor Moreno	Paz Vega
Evelyn Wright	Cloris Leachman
Cristina Moreno	Shelbie Bruce
Bernie Clasky	Sarah Steele
Georgie Clasky	Ian Hyland

Communication Concepts
Control and Power in Relationships
Defensive and Supportive Behaviors
Intercultural Communication
Relational Dialectics
Self-Concept and Identity Management

Viewing Information
This drama-comedy profiles a family with quite different spouses. John Clasky is a devoted and thoughtful father. John's wife, Deborah, is divisive and condescending. When the radiant Spanish-speaking Flor takes the job of family housekeeper, what follows is a lesson not only in intercultural communication but family values as well.

Synopsis

Spanglish opens with a scene at the Admissions office of Princeton University. In a voice-over, we learn that applicant Cristina Moreno identifies "the most influential person in her life" as her mother—Flor Moreno. What unfolds is a story about Flor's decision to work for an Anglo family, the Claskys, and how her choice changes their lives forever.

The Clasky family consists of father John, mother Deborah, their two children Bernie and Georgie, and Deborah's mother Evelyn Wright. Flor quickly discovers that John is a highly successful, and perhaps overly emotional, chef; Deborah is neurotic and hyper-competitive, lifting herself up by putting others down; Evelyn is an alcoholic, though kind and generous; and the children are desperate for the positive influence missing from their mother. When Flor and Cristina are forced to move in with the Claskys during the summer, Flor loses all sense of privacy and is on the verge of quitting the job. By the film's end, it's up to Flor to make decisions that at least provide a chance of the Claskys rebuilding their lives.

Discussion Questions

1. Identify and contrast examples of Gibb's categories for defensive and supportive behaviors displayed by the characters. What effects do these behaviors have on their relationships?
2. Identify examples of one-up and one-down messages. Which relationships are complementary? Which are symmetrical?
3. Which dialectical tensions do John and Flor experience, both with each other and independently? How do they choose to manage these tensions?
4. How do the characters influence each other's self-concept? What influence does culture have on this process?

STORIES WE TELL

Film Data	
Year	2012
Director	Sarah Polley
Length	108 minutes
Rating	PG-13

Main Cast	
Character	**Actor**
Sarah Polley	Herself
Michael Polley	Himself
Susy Buchan	Herself
John Buchan	Himself
Mark Polley	Himself
Joanna Polley	Herself

Communication Concepts
Identity/Self- Concept
Intimacy
Perception/perspectives
Relational Development

Viewing Information

   Stories We Tell is a documentary about director Sarah Polley's family, their memories of their mother, and how they each had their own take of the personalities and events of the past. Each family member is interviewed about their memories of growing up with their mother, and their recollections of the evolution of their family.

Synopsis

   Sarah Polley brings together her siblings to reminisce and share stories about their mother and their childhood. While their mother becomes a whole person through their stories, each person has their own take on their mother's personality and behaviors. Sarah also interviews her father, Michael Polley, and several other people from her mother's life, and the movie is brought together by the narration of Michael Polley's memoir.

Discussion Questions

1. Each child described their mother in slightly different terms, although each perspective came together to create the whole person. How did the perspectives differ? Why were they different?

2. Certain events were also described in very different terms. For example, Diane Polley's time in Montreal, and the time leading up to her death. What were the different stories? What did the stories say about the relationships each person had with Diane?

3. Within the film we get a closer look at the intimacy between Diane and Michael (her second husband), as well as the intimacy between Sarah and her father, Michael. What different types of intimacy were demonstrated? How did the intimacy develop?

THE THEORY OF EVERYTHING

Film Data	
Year	2014
Director	James Marsh
Length	123 minutes
Rating	PG-13

Main Cast	
Character	**Actor**
Stephen Hawking	Eddie Redmayne
Jane Hawking	Felicity Jones
Jonathan Jones	Charlie Cox
Dennis Sciama	David Thewlis

Communication Concepts
Intimacy
Identity/Self- Concept
Nonverbal Communication
Relational Development

Viewing Information

The Theory of Everything is an award-winning film adaptation of Jane Hawking's biography, focusing on the relationship between her and her famous physicist husband, Stephen Hawking. The film concentrates on the relationship between the two likable characters from their initial meeting at Oxford through Stephen's diagnosis with ALS and the progression of the disease. While the film does touch on some of Stephen Hawking's scientific work, it is not by any means a technically oriented film. The film is rated PG-13 for some language and adult themes.

Synopsis

Stephen Hawking was a young doctoral student studying physics at Cambridge in the 1960s when he met and fell in love with Jane. Not long after beginning their relationship, Stephen was diagnosed with ALS and given 2 years to live. Jane refused to give up on the relationship, and became not only Stephen's wife, but the mother of his three children and his caretaker as his physical situation declined. Through the film the two begin to drift apart, and end up divorcing after more than 20 years together.

Discussion Questions

1. We get to witness Stephen and Jane's relationship from initial encounter to dissolution of their marriage. Identify the key moments of Knapp's relational stages shown in the movie. What did they do (or not do) that allowed their relationship to progress to the next stages?

2. Jane's sense of identity appears to evolve over the time covered by the movie, from a poetry student to a young wife and mother, to a full-time nurse and caretaker, even handling Stephen's business affairs. Identify the points where Jane noticed the changes. How did she deal with them?

3. What types of intimacy were demonstrated throughout the film? How did the types of intimacy vary based on the relationships? How is intimacy a factor in the building or coming apart of relationships?

UP IN THE AIR

Film Data	
Year	2009
Director	Jason Reitman
Length	108 minutes
Rating	R

Main Cast	
Character	**Actor**
Ryan Bingham	George Clooney
Alex Goran	Vera Farmiga
Natalie Keener	Anna Kendrick
Craig Gregory	Jason Bateman
Bob	J.K. Simmons
Jim Miller	Danny McBride

Communication Concepts
Computer-Mediated Communication
Perspective Taking and Person-Centered Messages
Relational Commitment/Dialectics

Viewing Information
Ryan Bingham is a corporate downsizer who flies around the country firing people and avoiding relationships. Enter Natalie Keener, a feisty college graduate who wants to upend Ryan's business, and Alex Goran, an attractive business traveler who captures Ryan's heart. The results are a funny, ironic take on both romantic relationships and corporate culture. And as the title suggests, both women may indeed leave Ryan "up in the air."

Synopsis
Ryan Bingham is an island surrounded by a sea of travelers. Working for a company that specializes in corporate downsizing, Ryan is paid, essentially, to fire people. And apparently he is very good at what he does: Ryan's company flies him around the country over 300 days out of the year. He also gives motivational speeches about "relational downsizing," and living one's life out of a backpack—a metaphor for Ryan's lifestyle. Clearly more at home on the road, Ryan's way of life is threatened when the company hires Natalie Keener, an overly ambitious college graduate who wants to revolutionize his business: Natalie believes firing employees can be done through

teleconferencing and not in person. If that weren't threatening enough, Ryan begins a romantic relationship with fellow business traveler Alex, who causes him to question his self-imposed isolationism. Ryan Bingham might be an island, but he soon realizes that he is not alone.

Discussion Questions

1. Compare and contrast Natalie, Alex, and Ryan and their divergent views on relational commitment. How does each character define their romantic relationships? How do they manage the autonomy versus connection relational dialectic?
2. Analyze examples of person-centered messages Ryan creates as part of his job, and compare those with the messages he creates while not working. In which context is he more skilled at perspective taking? In which context is he more scripted?
3. Identify examples of computer-mediated communication (CMC) used throughout the film. In the business context, how effective is CMC? How do the characters use CMC outside of work?

SECTION IV
FEATURE FILM WEBSITES OF INTEREST

Now Playing Online
www.oup.com/us/nowplaying

Film Clips Online
www.filmclipsonline.com

Teach with Movies
www.teachwithmovies.org

Hartwick Classic Film Leadership Cases
http://www.hartwickinstitute.org/Store.aspx?Action=Sort&Type=Film

The Internet Movie Database
www.imdb.com

Film.Com
www.film.com

Movie Review Query Engine
www.mrqe.com

Roger Ebert Reviews
rogerebert.suntimes.com

INDEX BY COMMUNICATION CONCEPTS